Governing at the Top

Other Books by the Author

Eight Keys to an Extraordinary Board-Superintendent Partnership
Extraordinary Board Leadership: The Governing Keys to High-Impact Governance
Five Habits of High-Impact School Boards
The Board-Savvy Superintendent

Governing at the Top

Building a Board-Superintendent
Strategic Governing Team

Doug Eadie

ROWMAN & LITTLEFIELD
Lanham • Boulder • New York • Toronto • Plymouth, UK

Published by Rowman & Littlefield
4501 Forbes Boulevard, Suite 200, Lanham, Maryland 20706
www.rowman.com

10 Thornbury Road, Plymouth PL6 7PP, United Kingdom

British Library Cataloguing in Publication Information Available

Library of Congress Cataloging-in-Publication Data

Library of Congress Cataloging-in-Publication Data Is Available.
ISBN 978-1-4758-0715-8 (cloth : alk. paper) — ISBN 978-1-4758-0716-5 (pbk. : alk. paper) —
ISBN 978-1-4758-0717-2 (electronic)

♾️™ The paper used in this publication meets the minimum requirements of American
National Standard for Information Sciences Permanence of Paper for Printed Library
Materials, ANSI/NISO Z39.48-1992.

Printed in the United States of America

To
The Vandalia Community Schools
Vandalia, Illinois

And In Memory Of
Superintendent G. V. Blythe

Contents

Foreword

Over the course of our careers in public education, we have learned that if you come across a school board that is doing truly high-impact governing work—setting clear strategic directions, effectively addressing high-stakes issues, making well-informed and timely governing decisions, and the like—you can be sure that the board is working hand-in-hand with, and receiving strong support from, a superintendent who is what author Doug Eadie calls "board-savvy." And if you encounter a superintendent whose chief executive leadership is making a tremendous positive difference in her district, you can count on there being a supportive, collaborative school board backing her up. Experience has taught us that the long-term success of a public school system—in terms of educational, financial, and administrative performance and of community support—heavily depends on a rock-solid board-superintendent partnership that is up to the challenge of governing in these rapidly changing times. That partnership is essentially what this important new book is all about.

Governing at the Top: Building a High-Impact Board-Superintendent Strategic Governing Team is a unique addition to the literature of K–12 governance in many respects. In chapter 1, author Doug Eadie sets the stage for what follows by offering a crystal-clear, eminently practical definition of the work of governing that goes well beyond the old-time, static notion of governing as merely "policy making." The nuts and bolts work of governing, according to Doug, involves the school board—in close partnership with its superintendent and executive team—in making a never-ending stream of decisions about very concrete governing "products," such as an updated values and vision statement and the annual operating plan. And he suggests that developing and fine-tuning the processes for making these governing decisions is one of the preeminent keys to effective school board leadership.

Doug's detailed description in chapter 2 of the role that a "board-savvy" superintendent plays as an integral partner with the school board on what Doug calls the "Strategic Governing Team" is another unique feature of this powerful new book. A true expert in the rapidly changing field of public/nonprofit governance, the board-savvy superintendent plays a leading role in helping her board develop its governing capacity and takes the lead in mapping out processes for proactive, meaningful board engagement in making governing decisions and judgments. Doug goes on in chapter 3 to provide practical, detailed guidance to school boards and superintendents in developing the board's governing capacity by updating what he calls the board's "governing architecture:" its overall governing role; the people serving on the board; and the structure that organizes the board's governing work. And in chapter 4, Doug explores in detail how well-designed board standing committees can serve as "continuous governing improvement vehicles," fine-tuning board involvement in the key governing areas of planning, performance monitoring, and external relations.

Finally, far from being just another one of those surveys of the various theoretical governance "models" floating around in the literature, *Governing at the Top* is truly a practitioner-focused book that draws on Doug's extensive, real-life experience of over a quarter-century of work with hundreds of boards and chief executives. Board members, superintendents, and senior executives in school districts of all sizes will find this book a treasure-trove of very practical guidance that they can put to good use in meeting whatever governing challenges they face.

Bruce Caughey
Executive Director, Colorado Association of School Executives
Robert Rader
Executive Director, Connecticut Association of Boards of Education

Acknowledgments

As I meandered through the waterfront park near my home a few weeks ago, taking a break from writing the manuscript of this book, it came to me how fortunate—and how privileged—I was to be writing a book dealing with a critical facet of an enterprise that I am passionate about and that is one of America's most precious resources: our public schools. Reflecting on my good fortune got me thinking about my own public school education in Vandalia, Illinois, a lovely town of around 7,000 at the northern tip of southern Illinois, around seventy miles east of St. Louis. Walking along, recalling teachers who'd loomed so large in my life back then in Vandalia, I realized how indebted I am to the Vandalia Community Schools. It gives me great pleasure to retire that debt in part by dedicating this book to the public school system where I spent twelve very happy years, preparing for the journey I was destined to travel, and to the memory of Superintendent G. V. Blythe, a superb leader and wise mentor.

I am only the primary author of this book. My coauthors are the many school board members, superintendents, and senior administrators I have worked with over the years, who have taught me the lessons that I share in the following pages. I especially want to thank Bruce Caughey, executive director of the Colorado Association of School Executives, and Rick Lewis, executive director of the Ohio School Boards Association, whose associations organized and hosted teleconferences for the purpose of providing me with practitioner feedback on this book's key concepts and structure. The school board members, superintendents, and senior administrators who participated in the CASE and OSBA teleconferences deserve my sincere thanks for helping to make this book a more robust leadership resource. Representing Colorado are: Mark DeVoti, assistant executive director, Colorado Association of School Boards; Superintendent Ranelle Lang, Greeley 6; Superintendent Scott Mader, South Routt RE-3; Superintendent Glenn McClain, Platte Valley RE-7; Superintendent Bruce Messinger, Boulder Valley RE-2; Superintendent Randy Miller, Eaton RE-2; Superintendent Carol Noll, East Otero R-1; Superintendent Michael Page, Springfield RE-4; Superintendent Kevin Schott, North Conejos RE-1J; Superintendent Thomas Turrell, Byers 32-J; Superintendent Richard Walter, Miami/Yoder 60-JT; and Superintendent George Welsh, Center 26-JT. Representing Ohio are: Damon Asbury, director, Legislative Services, Ohio School Boards Association; Lock Beachum Sr., board member, Youngstown City Schools; Marguerite Bennett, board president, Mount Vernon City Schools; Dawn Burks, board president, Rossford Exempted Village Schools; Tim Cleary, board president, Winton Woods City Schools; Marie Dockry, board member, Mahoning County ESC and Mahoning County Career and Technical Center; Michael Hogan, board member, Chagrin Falls Exempted Village Schools; Kathy LaSota, director, Board Services, Ohio School Boards Association; Susan Lawson, board member, Tri-County ESC and Wayne County Career Center; Karen Mantia, superintendent, Lakota Local Schools; John Marschhausen, superintendent, Hilliard City Schools; Gail Martindale, board member, Cedar Cliff Local Schools; Katie McNeil, board member, Middletown City Schools and Butler County Career and Technical Center; Deborah Piotrowski, superintendent, Xenia City Schools; Cheryl Ryan, deputy director, Board Services, Ohio School Boards Association; Joe Shucofsky, board president, Fairview Park City Schools; Kay VanHo, board president, Euclid City Schools; Charlie Wilson, president, Board of Trustees, Ohio School Boards Association, and board member, Worthington City Schools.

As always, Tom Koerner, vice president and publisher, Rowman & Littlefield, deserves my appreciation for his encouragement, support, and insightful advice and counsel during the writing of this book. I also want to acknowledge the very capable support I received from Karen Ackermann, assistant managing editor, and Carlie Wall, assistant editor, of Rowman & Littlefield.

Finally, I could not have written nearly as good a book without the loving support and the always thoughtful and occasionally challenging input of my best friend and wife, Barbara Carlson Krai. Thank you once again, Barbara.

Of course, I am solely responsible for any shortcomings the reader might find in this book.

Chapter One

The Wild and Wonderful World of Governing

MEETING THE GOVERNING CHALLENGE

This book is about the keys to building the kind of high-impact governing partnership between your school district's board and your superintendent that will make a significant difference in your district's affairs over the long haul—in terms of educational performance (especially student achievement), administrative effectiveness, and financial stability—and will stand the test of time, no matter what issues you've got to grapple with in the future. My aim is to provide you with detailed, thoroughly tested guidance that you can put to immediate use in your school district to build the kind of rock-solid partnership these really challenging times demand. You can think of this book as a high-level practitioner resource that's based on real life nuts and bolts best practices, not on abstract governing theory. A good place to begin our exploration of the keys to board-superintendent partnership-building is to reflect on the governing challenge that contemporary public school districts face and then to take a brief a tour of the fascinating and highly complex terrain of K–12 governing, looking at the nature of your school board and the work it does when it governs.

"You've been working with all kinds of nonprofit and public boards, Doug, for at least a couple of decades. Would you say there are particular kinds of boards that have an especially tough row to hoe—certain organizations that are really hard to govern?" I'm paraphrasing the question a young woman asked a few weeks ago at a governance workshop I was presenting in Chicago. It wasn't the first time I'd heard the question, so I wasn't caught totally off guard, and I definitely thought it was a good question that deserved a serious response. I began by pointing out that doing a good job of governing any nonprofit or public organization—whether in education, health care, social services, or another sector—was a tremendous challenge under the most favorable circumstances, requiring lots of thinking and planning. I'd learned early in my career that getting a well-intentioned, dedicated, bright and energetic group of volunteers together in the boardroom wasn't close to half the battle. Good governing wouldn't automatically happen, no matter how qualified the cast of characters sitting at the board table. That said, I told my workshop participants that near the top of my list of difficult-to-govern organizations would be public school districts, for a number of reasons that I briefly described. I'd like to share some of what appear to be the most important ones before taking you on a tour of the K–12 governance terrain.

School districts aren't alone in being a tough nut to crack where governing is concerned, of course. Based on my experience, public transportation authorities and national trade associations are also high on the scale of governance difficulty. But the governing challenges public school systems face appear uniquely daunting to me. For one thing, I can't imagine being accountable for carrying out a more complex, high-stakes mission than the one guiding our public schools. To start with, our public schools' primary "customer"—the student—is also the primary "product." Of course, school districts have plenty of indirect customers, including parents and taxpayers generally, but the core customer sits in the classroom and over the course of, hopefully, twelve years, presumably becomes a significantly different person, at least in terms of knowledge and intellectual skills. And what a customer: not only incredibly diverse and becoming more so by the day, but also in many cases a reluctant and sometimes even unwilling customer who would rather be anywhere else than in the classroom. And the ultimate "product" our public school districts are expected to produce—an educated student—couldn't be more complex and difficult to measure. Even with the accountability thrust in recent years and the growing reliance on standardized tests to measure educational performance and student achievement, the K–12 "production process" is still as much art as science.

Yes, school districts these days, responding to federal and state government directions, do a pretty good job of measuring basic math and English competence at particular points in their students' academic journeys, but few would disagree that focusing on the so-called "basics" doesn't come close to accomplishing the full educational mission of a public school district. What about such notoriously difficult-to-measure outcomes of the educational process as preparing our student customers to thrive in an ever more rapidly changing and challenging world, about transforming our student customers into good citizens with solid values who care deeply about the welfare of the communities they live and work in, and about fostering the creative capacity of our students? When we go beyond the barebones educational basics, *what* should be measured is just as thorny a question as *how* to go about measuring it. By contrast, public transportation authority boards I've worked with over the years can be pretty confident about the objective, measurable outcomes they're accountable for producing, such as ridership and on-time performance. And trade association performance metrics are pretty standard: membership numbers; attendance at the annual meeting and educational programs, and the like.

I'm reminded of a column I wrote a year or so ago that appeared in the *American School Board Journal*. A wonderful public high school teacher, James Thornton, had recently died and the memorial Facebook page his former students had put up quickly filled with dozens of moving testimonials. Mr. Thornton—"JT" to many of his students and colleagues—created, developed, and, for almost a quarter-century, headed the nationally recognized Theatre Arts Department at Shaker Heights High School in that lovely suburban community on the southeast border of Cleveland, Ohio. Mr. Thornton without question nurtured the creative capacity of hundreds of students over the years, including my daughter Jennifer and son William. My kids are both highly successful attorneys who, along with many other alumni of Mr. Thornton's theater arts program, passionately believe that their professional success owes a tremendous amount to Mr. Thornton's helping them to develop their creative capacity. The question I posed in my column is just as pertinent for K–12 leaders today:

> This column talks about a wonderful human being and extraordinary teacher who left a legacy of fuller, richer, more successful lives: the best definition of the educational mission I know of. But James Thornton's profound educational impact came from a theater arts program that many people around the country would describe as "extra-curricular"—outside of the "core" curriculum—and, for many, an expensive luxury rather than an essential academic offering. And even more worrisome in this era of accountability, with its emphasis on measurable, testable results, JT's profound, life-transforming impacts largely defy measurement. But let me close by suggesting that what happened under James Thornton's leadership and continues to happen today at the Shaker Heights Theatre Arts Department is as educationally hard core and basic—as essential and far from being a luxury—as anything in the educational enterprise can be. How can you, sitting in your boardrooms, factor the Shaker experience into your governing decisions? This is the profoundly important question I leave you with.

If governing a public educational enterprise with such a complex, multifaceted mission weren't challenge enough, political, cultural, and market-related factors make the work of governing K–12 systems even more difficult in today's world. For one thing, school districts typically loom large in their communities, often making the top ten in terms of capital assets, employment, and operating budgets. Being one of the big community kahunas definitely has its advantages—for example, entitling your public school district to a seat at the community-wide decision-making table in areas like community and economic development planning. But in these times of widespread and apparently growing skepticism and distrust of large institutions, looming large on the community landscape can come at a stiff price: unremitting, and all-too-often negative, public scrutiny, forcing districts to divert precious attention and other resources to aggressive public relations strategies and making fund-raising (whether passing a tax increase or building an endowment to fund innovation) extremely difficult.

Despite the steadily growing skepticism and suspicion about the motives and effectiveness of large public institutions, it doesn't appear that parents and other community residents expect less from their local school districts. On the contrary, ever faster paced lives and the steady increase in two-career families mean that we expect schools to handle a growing part of the traditional parental burden of character building and, although probably a lost cause, insulating students from the pervasive and often dangerous influence of the social media. And the educational "marketplace," as everyone knows, has become much more competitive in recent years, expanding parent choice and forcing districts to demonstrate their effectiveness and pay close attention to public relations and marketing—or risk enrollment decline and diminished revenues.

WHAT EXACTLY IS YOUR GOVERNING BOARD?

So much for why public school districts are a uniquely tough governing challenge. Now, what about the body that has been charged—formally and legally—to carry out the difficult work of governing: your school board? Let's begin by defining what, generally speaking, a governing board is. You might not have thought about it this way, but, by definition, your school district's board is, like every other governing board, an organization within the umbrella of your district's wider organizational structure. It's a formally established, permanent organizational unit consisting of people who are dedicated to carrying out a common mission and who work together according to a formal set of policies.

So your school board is an example of the many organizational units that make up your district structure, such as the office of the superintendent, the financial services department, every one of your schools, the office of curriculum and instruction, and so on. Of course, your board is a very special organizational unit in terms of its formal authority, its influence on district directions, and its tremendously complex and high-stakes governing mission. Now, when you pause to think about it, you'll realize that, like any other organizational unit in your district, your board can be consciously, systematically developed to strengthen its capacity to accomplish its mission. I'll talk about that in real detail in chapter 3, which deals with what I call "board design," but for now let's continue our exploration of the nature of your board and its work.

THE WORK YOUR BOARD DOES

Yes, your board is just another one of many organizational units making up your district, but what hits you in the face is how unique and high-stakes its work is. Consisting in the great majority of cases of unpaid, elected volunteers, the great majority of whom are not professional educators, your district's board has one preeminent mission that is critical to your district's long-term success: *to govern your district.* So what do we mean by "governing?" Since public and nonprofit boards have been around for over a century in this country, governing hospitals, colleges, social service agencies, transportation authorities, as well as every one of the nation's public school systems, you'd think that the work of governing would be well-defined and universally understood by this time. Well, you'd be wrong.

Wearing my consultant hat, I've interviewed hundreds of board members involved in public education among many other sectors for the past quarter-century, usually as a key part of preparing for an upcoming board-chief executive retreat. One of the questions I always ask is: "What exactly do you and your board colleagues do when you govern? Tell me about your governing work in detail." I can count the number of really comprehensive, detailed answers on one hand. More often than not, I hear something vague like: "We're the policy makers," or "We set overall directions," or "We make sure staff are achieving their objectives and doing a good job," or "We oversee the whole shebang."

Probing for more detail doesn't usually get me very far. Based on this experience, I've concluded that many, if not most, board members—whether they're seasoned veterans or newcomers to the board room—don't really have a very detailed grasp of their governing mission. I've never spent time trying to determine why there's such widespread ignorance about the detailed governing work that boards do, but my guess is that most people think of governing as amateur work that anyone can do, as contrasted with the highly technical executive work involved in running a school district, which obviously requires well-educated professionals. Allow me to share my definition of what it means to govern, based on my observations of hundreds of boards over the past twenty-five years.

AT THE HIGHEST LEVEL

At the highest level, what your school board does when it governs is continuously answer three very fundamental questions that are never answered definitively, for all time, because your district's internal and external circumstances are always evolving in this rapidly changing world:

1. What do we want our district to become over the long run, in terms of our educational achievement, our leadership, our financial situation, our reputation and community support, our internal culture, etc.? You can think of this as the strategic question, which involves some kind of strategic planning process that engages our board in updating values and vision and setting strategic targets.
2. What is our district now and in the near term in terms of our mission, annual educational performance goals, staffing level, budget, operating policies, management structure, etc.? You can think of this as the operational planning question, which engages our board in some kind of operational planning and annual budget development process within the context of our mission.
3. And the third major governing question that your board answers over and over again is: How is our district doing, in terms of educational, managerial, and financial performance and our relationships with the community-at-large and key stakeholders, including the parents of our students? This is the accountability question, which as you well know, is closest to the heart of our community's taxpayers, who have become increasingly skeptical of public institutions, including school districts. Our board answers this question by determining the content and format of performance reports, reviewing the information in the reports, and making judgments about our district's performance along various lines.

DRILLING DOWN

These three questions might seem pretty abstract and theoretical, but there's nothing very ethereal about the nuts and bolts work of governing that's involved in answering these questions over and over again. Of course, they're never definitively answered, for all time, because circumstances are always changing, requiring, for example, that visions and strategic goals be updated periodically and operational plans and budgets be adjusted annually. At a detailed level, what your board does when it governs is make decisions about very concrete governing "products" and judgments based on concrete information supplied to your board. These decisions and judgments flow along three broad governing streams:

1. Strategic and operational planning/budget development
2. Performance monitoring
3. External/stakeholder relations

Since I discuss in detail how your board and superintendent can work together as a cohesive high-impact governing team in mapping out processes for board engagement in these governing streams, in chapters 4, let me just give some brief examples here of what I mean by governing decisions and judgments:

- Your board's planning and development committee, after a highly participatory six-month process involving input from administrators, faculty members, and community representatives, has put the updated district values and vision statement on the agenda of the upcoming board meeting. When the board adopts the vision and values statement, it will have made a very important governing decision about one of the most important governing products. Calling the values and vision statement a "governing product" doesn't mean only the board was involved in developing it, of course—just that it requires a board decision.
- Your board's performance monitoring committee, over the course of two lengthy work sessions, has pored over the report of the faculty committee that carried out an exhaustive assessment of the pilot community engagement process our district has been testing over the past six months, and the committee has concluded (made a governing judgment) that four of the engagement strategies have been really productive and worth continuing but that the fifth hasn't had much positive impact and most likely shouldn't be carried forward.
- Your board's external/stakeholder relations committee will be recommending a comprehensive stakeholder relations strategy at the next board meeting, specifying how board members should be involved in maintaining the district's relationships with the highest priority stakeholders. When the board approves this strategy, it will be making a governing decision.

That's it; that's governing work in the nutshell—nothing theoretically fancy, just nuts and bolts judgments and decisions. I'm not suggesting that the work is simple to accomplish, or that the board could do it alone. The examples I've given obviously involve considerable staff work and extensive board deliberations before the judgments and decisions were made. But the literal work of governing isn't at all complex, conceptually speaking. I often use the term "high-impact governing" in the following pages, so I'd like to define it briefly here. I don't mean that high-impact governing work is different in kind; it still involves making continuous judgments and decisions. But two characteristics make it different from run of the mill governing work. First, it deals with the highest stakes issues facing a school district (meaning that the district will pay a stiff penalty by not dealing with the issue, such as losing a large foundation grant or suffering significant enrollment and revenue decline). And second, as a consequence, high-impact governing work makes a tremendous difference in the affairs of your district, in terms of, for example, educational performance, financial stability, and community support.

BUT WHAT ABOUT POLICY MAKING?

When your board adopts an updated or completely new policy, it's obviously making a decision about a governing product, no question. What you need to keep in mind, however, is that policy making per se is a relatively small part of the governing puzzle, requiring on the average, I'd estimate, between 5 and 10 percent of your board's time. Policies are essentially broad rules governing your school district's operations, which are developed within the overall framework of state laws and regulations, and several of these rules are important enough to merit serious board attention: for example, setting school boundaries and starting and ending times; spelling out the superintendent's latitude in signing contracts and checks without board approval; determining how vendors will be selected; establishing ethical guidelines for board members, including defining conflicts of interest and how to handle them .

Once your district has a comprehensive set of rules—or policies—covering the various educational and administrative functions of your district, periodically fashioning new policies and adopting updated versions of one policy or another are typically a small part of your board's ongoing governing work. Granted, there will be times when a new or updated policy is so complex—technically and/or politically—that the board has to spend substantial time on it. To take a recent example I'm familiar with, a proposed policy setting the high school starting time an hour later brought many inconvenienced parents out of the woodwork and required board members to spend hours in public hearings. But this kind of thing is definitely the exception to the rule.

It's also important for you to keep in mind that knowing the rules of a game—the boundaries, how scoring is done, what constitutes a foul, etc.— obviously doesn't get the game played. The same is true of your school district. Having a comprehensive, meticulously developed set of policies that's been adopted by your school board won't get your educational programs carried out or operate your buildings. Your school board has many more decisions and judgments to make that go well beyond the rules of the educational game.

BOARDS DO NONGOVERNING WORK, TOO

Governing as I've defined it isn't the only work that nonprofit and public boards do. Many boards involve their members in doing important work that doesn't involve making governing judgments and decisions, as I discuss in detail in chapter 4. To take some real-life school district examples, school board members around the country often represent their board colleagues at graduation exercises and other important district events; make presentations about district accomplishments and issues in important civic forums, such as Rotary Club and chamber of commerce luncheons; serve on the boards of important district stakeholders, such as the regional economic development commission; and testify before state legislative committees, among other non-governing activities.

There's absolutely nothing wrong with board members engaging in important non-governing work, provided that they are needed and well-qualified to do work that is important to the district's mission. Indeed, many school districts and other nonprofit and public clients I've worked with have specified in their board governing missions (which is what descriptions of board governing functions are often called) some of the more critical non-governing board member responsibilities. However, be aware of the clear and present danger than this kind of "doing" work can all too easily detract from the board's preeminent function: to govern. Never underestimate how powerful the siren song of interesting, ego-satisfying, and even fun non-governing work can be, especially when contrasted with the often grueling work of making tough governing decisions. In a school board-superintendent governance work session I was facilitating a little over a year ago, one of our breakout groups reported to the assembled district leaders that assigning board members to serve as liaisons to various critical stakeholder organizations in the community, such as the mayor's office, county commission, educational foundation, and regional planning commission, while useful, was consuming an inordinate amount of the time board members could reasonably be expected to contribute to district affairs, making it extremely difficult to find the time to participate in such critical governing work as the annual daylong strategic planning work session.

GOVERNING IS A TEAM ENDEAVOR

Up to now, I've focused on the nature of school boards and their governing role, but long experience has taught me that the kind of high-impact governing performance that makes a significant difference in the affairs of a school district is the product of what I call the district's Strategic Governing Team, consisting of your board of education and your district's chief executive officer. Both partners bring essential resources to this governing partnership. Starting on the board side of the governing equation, first and foremost, your board of education brings to the table the formal authority required to make governing decisions—and to make occasional—and inevitable—controversial decisions stick in the face of even strident opposition. This formal—indeed legal—authority includes what is traditionally one of the preeminent legislative prerequisites in all public and nonprofit organizations: power of the purse, most notably the authority to adopt the long-range capital and the annual operating budgets. This is why many commentators have called the annual budget one of the foremost board governing products and, consequently, a strong argument for involving your board meaningfully and early in shaping your district's annual budget.

Your school board is also a powerful potential contributor to your district's process for making strategic decisions about complex and high-stakes issues that can't be handled effectively through the annual operational planning process—a role I've described as the "gold standard" for school board involvement in governing. In addition to the formal authority to make high-level, long-term planning decisions, your board members are a precious asset in terms of the accumulated knowledge, experience, expertise, and perspectives they bring to the planning process. One of the major reasons, by the way, that day-long retreats involving the board, superintendent, and executive team have become so popular as a planning vehicle is that they provide a wonderful opportunity for board members to bring all of their accumulated experience and wisdom to bear in shaping strategic decisions, rather than merely reacting to executive-prepared strategies. Facilitating such planning sessions over the years, I've often been amazed by the powerful contribution board members can make to the strategic decision making process, particularly in assessing the implications of major conditions and trends (such as a community's evolving demographic mix and economic development) and the identification of high-stakes issues in the form of both challenges and opportunities (such as emerging new needs because of demographic and economic change).

And your school board, wearing its representative hat, also brings to the boardroom valuable connections to important constituencies and stakeholders in your community. Too often, I'm sorry to say, these precious community links are seen in problematic terms, rather than as a precious asset in the governing process: the specter of school board members bringing a single-constituency mindset to decision making, rather than being open-minded. This can happen, of course, but such community connections are nonetheless invaluable in decision making. They not only ensure that public opinion is factored into decision making (for example, anticipating opposition from certain segments of your community and strategizing how to neutralize it), they also provide communication channels for explaining complex decisions before they are finalized and battle lines have hardened. It's always advisable to keep in mind that when governing decisions have significant direct external impact (for example, policies to govern the use of district buildings), support from key constituencies and stakeholders can be a critical part of getting such decisions implemented without needless turmoil. By the way, by "stakeholder," I mean any formal group or organization in your community with which it makes sense for your district to maintain some kind of relationship because of the stakes involved.

On the executive side of the governing equation, your superintendent— and by extension her top lieutenants comprising your district's senior administrative or executive team—bring much more to the governing process than just the old-fashioned notion that the preeminent role of executives, administrators, and other staff is to execute governing decisions that your board has made. To be sure, the superintendent and his executives are ultimately the organizational engine that translates board decisions into practice, but high-impact governing is heavily dependent on your superintendent and staff being intimately involved in the governing process from beginning to end. This will be pretty obvious when you think about it. What will probably come immediately to mind is the fact that, as your district's chief executive officer, the superintendent has access to—and brings to the board room—the educational, financial, and other information that your board needs to make informed, intelligent governing decisions. But the executive role in governing goes well beyond that simple and obvious responsibility.

For example, only your superintendent and her top lieutenants are able to come up with the time, knowledge, and expertise to help your board put in place the structure (such as well-designed standing committees) and the processes (such as the annual operational planning and budget preparation procedures and the daylong retreat kicking off your district's strategic decision making process) that will enable the board to play a meaningful role in making governing decisions. Your board members couldn't be expected to play this expert role successfully. And only your superintendent and her senior administrators are in a position to provide the support necessary to make the moving parts of your district's governing structure and processes work. I'll illustrate the point with a recent real-life experience. When the planning committee of the board of one of my school district clients concurred with the superintendent's recommendation that they hold a daylong retreat, the superintendent and two of her top administrators followed up by bringing to the next planning committee meeting a recommended detailed design for bringing off a successful retreat, dealing with such critical elements as the mechanism for developing the detailed agenda, potential retreat locations, how professional facilitation would be handled, and what follow-up steps would be needed. And, of course, the superintendent and her executive team provided strong support to the ad hoc retreat planning committee that was established to develop the agenda and to select the facilitator.

Finally, keep in mind that superintendents who are what I call "board-savvy" tend to make for much stronger partners with the board in governing. Chapter 2 describes the characteristics of board-savvy superintendents in detail, including seeing the school board as a precious asset, welcoming strong board leadership, being committed to working in partnership with the board, making the governing function a top-tier chief executive priority, and taking the lead in developing the board's governing capacity. Since a superintendent's lacking board savvy-ness is, in my experience, one of the major reasons why board-superintendent partnerships erode—and hence why superintendents lose their jobs—it makes the best of sense for superintendents to make a concerted effort to beef up their governing IQ.

A FRAGILE PARTNERSHIP IN THE BEST OF TIMES

Over the years I've come across enough badly frayed board-superintendent partnerships to wonder if a really rock-solid working relationship that can stand the test of challenging times is the exception that proves the rule that board-superintendent partnerships are extremely fragile—and prone to unravel alarmingly quickly. That's not very surprising when you think about it. In the first place, the cast of characters comprising your district's Strategic Governing Team makes for a pretty volatile mix of people who are notoriously resistant to being melded into a cohesive governing team: high-achieving, ambitious, egotistical, strong-willed, and more often than not classic "Type A" personalities. When you add to this volatile mix the pressures and stresses and strains at the top of any large, complex enterprise like a school district that, in these rapidly changing times, is constantly bombarded with complex, high-stakes issues, it's nothing short of miraculous that so many board-superintendent relationships endure as long as they do.

One thing for sure: taking the board-superintendent working relationship for granted would be a perilous course of action, at least for superintendents. Conscious, systematic management and maintenance of the relationship are required to keep it healthy, as I'll explore in chapter 6.

COMMON BARRIERS TO HIGH-IMPACT GOVERNING

I've learned that it makes the best of sense to go into any game with your eyes wide open, understanding that no matter how talented, motivated and dedicated you and your teammates are, you need to anticipate obstacles to winning and pay close attention to how you can overcome them. This is certainly true of the governing game, which involves not only a potentially volatile group of participants, but also tremendously complex and high-stakes work. So let's look briefly at some of the more serious barriers to high-impact governing that I've observed over the years and that the practical guidance in the following pages is aimed at helping you overcome, starting with some built-in problems with your school board organization itself.

In my writing and speaking over the years, I've made the point that governing is a function, like chief executive-ship, that transcends particular kinds of nonprofit and public organizations, and that the boards that carry out the governing function in diverse sectors such as education, social services, health care, and public transportation are much more alike than different. That said, it's important to keep in mind as we traverse the K–12 governance terrain that there are three unique structural and cultural features that distinguish school boards from many other nonprofit and public governing boards and that, in my opinion, work against effective governance:

First, the great majority of school boards are quite small when compared to other nonprofit and public boards—between five and nine members. Although I've heard consultants and teachers tout the benefits of small boards: principally that they work more efficiently as governing mechanisms—having an easier time reaching consensus and making final decisions—and that their deliberations are easier to manage and support. These minor efficiency benefits are, in my experience, outweighed by significant costs.

For one thing, smaller, less diverse boards bring less experience, knowledge, expertise, and perspectives to the process of making complex governing judgments and decisions. For another, smaller school boards reduce ties to the wider community, making public and stakeholder relations an even more challenging function. And, of special interest to superintendents, a small board is much more vulnerable to being highjacked by a single-issue, ax-grinding contingent that is all-too-often pledged to ousting the chief executive. I've seen this happen more than once in recent years, primarily as a result of the culture wars that we continue to wage. I saw this firsthand a couple of years ago, when four newly elected members of a seven-member school board were passionately united on a particular issue: removing "inappropriate" books from the two middle school libraries. Being closely tied to the former, more broad-minded majority, the superintendent found herself in a perilous situation that she was barely able to survive.

Second, being for the most part elected boards that do not nominate candidates for vacant positions, school boards tend to have little or no influence on board composition, which removes one of the important levers for board capacity building in the wider nonprofit world. By contrast, many nonprofits I work with whose boards are self-appointing pay close attention to filling their own vacancies, typically by reaching agreement on the most desirable board member attributes and qualifications (such as having prior successful board experience and having demonstrated open-mindedness) and using this profile to recruit new members. And many of my association clients whose boards are elected by their membership employ a nominating committee to identify qualified candidates to fill vacancies. I know of one school board that supports an independent blue ribbon citizen panel responsible for screening school board candidates and promoting their election, but I'm sure this is the rare exception that proves the rule.

The former two characteristics are obviously structural and beyond the direct control of the school board. They're facts of life in the K–12 governance world that you've got to cope with since you can't really change them. The third, however, being cultural, is amenable to change: the adversarial, watch-the-critters-so-they-don't-steal-the-store tradition. In my twenty-five years of work with nonprofit and public boards of all shapes and sizes, I've never encountered a stronger we-they tradition than in public education governance. The absence of trust and the in-built tension between the school board, on the one hand, and the superintendent and her top administrators, on the other, is often palpable, making good governance far more difficult to achieve. That's the bad news. The better news is that cultural change is always possible when the parties are committed to accomplishing it. Here are some other barriers that might hinder your district in developing a high-impact Strategic Governing Team:

- Your superintendent isn't sufficiently board-savvy, not bringing the right attitude to his work with the school board, not being knowledgeable enough about the work of nonprofit and public governing, and not recognizing the need to handle the human dimension of the board-superintendent governing partnership.
- Your school board is under-developed as a governing organization, lacking a well-defined governing role or mission, a systematic process for developing board member governing knowledge and expertise, and a contemporary, well-designed committee structure.
- Your school board is under-managed as a governing body, meaning that the board does not set clear governing performance targets, monitor its own governing performance, or systematically correct governing deficiencies.
- The processes for involving board members in a meaningful fashion in key governing areas such as strategic and operational planning and performance monitoring are under-designed, leaving board members dissatisfied and frustrated by their lack of engagement that makes a difference.
- The board-superintendent working relationship is taken for granted and allowed to erode, rather than being meticulously and systematically managed to keep it healthy.

What have I missed? I'm pretty sure that more than one of you reading this will say, "What about school board members themselves, Doug? You've already made the point that they're for the most part elected without the benefit of some kind of nominating process that screens for desirable attributes and qualifications. In light of this near-total lack of quality control over the board's composition, isn't one of the most important potential barriers a school board with several members, if not a majority, who are really unqualified to do high-impact governing?" Well, to take a clear stand on the issue, I'll say "yes" and "no." Yes, experience has taught me that you're quite right that newly elected board members are very likely not to be prepared to do a bang-up job of governing your district; there's a good chance they won't bring a positive, team-spirited attitude or much expertise in the details of governing to the boardroom.

But, no, that doesn't need to be a serious barrier, since your board can take many practical steps—which you'll read about in the following pages—to re-shape attitudes and bring board members up to speed in the governing business. Of course, you'll encounter occasional bad apples that are impervious to improvement efforts, but long experience has made me an optimist. I've learned that the great majority of board members arrive in the boardroom sincerely wanting to do a good job, because they really do believe in public education, and that they are basically capable of doing a solid job of governing. However, bringing them up to full speed in the governing business will very likely require a large dollop of well-designed orientation and training, along with carefully crafted governing structure and process for involving them actively in governing. That's what much of this book is about.

COMING EVENTS

Having taken this brief tour of the nonprofit and public governing terrain—looking at the nature of your board as a governing organization, going beyond the simplistic notion of "policy-making" in exploring the work of governing, defining what the partners making up your district's Strategic Governing Team bring to the governing game, and considering some potholes you might encounter on the governing road—we can now move on in the following four chapters to address the key elements involved in building a truly high-impact Strategic Governing Team:

Chapter 2: Your Governing Lynchpin—the Board-Savvy Superintendent takes a close look at the role of the superintendent as your district's "Board Ally-in-Chief"—in terms of bringing the right attitude to the governing arena; making governing a top-tier chief executive priority; playing the lead role in the ongoing design of the board as a governing organization, wearing the "Chief Board

Developer" hat; taking the lead in mapping out processes for meaningful board member engagement in key governing areas, such as strategic and operational planning, wearing the "Chief Process Designer" hat; and ensuring that the board-superintendent working relationship is well-managed.

Chapter 3: Designing Your Board As a Governing Organization describes how your district's board and superintendent can work closely together in developing your board's governing capacity by updating the board's governing design, in terms of the people serving on the board, the board's governing role, and its governing structure; examines resistance to systematically developing your board's governing capacity and how it might be overcome; describes two powerful approaches to updating your board's governing design that have proved useful in practice; and then takes a close look at how school districts have strengthened their board as a human resource, clarified the board's role, and updated its structure.

Chapter 4: Board Engagement In Governing Work describes how your superintendent can work closely with your board's standing committees in updating processes for involving board members in key governing processes, such as planning and performance monitoring so as to generate sound governing outcomes while also fostering board member ownership of the outcomes; examines real-life cases of board engagement; and devotes detailed attention to involving board members in the "governing gold standard:" leading out of the box change in the educational enterprise; and takes a look at important non-governing work that the school board might legitimately do.

Chapter 5: Maintaining a Healthy Board-Superintendent Working Relationship examines the fragile nature of this key district relationship; describes important elements involved in maintaining a healthy relationship, including a dedicated board committee, guidelines for board-superintendent communication and interaction, and ground rules for board interaction with executive staff under the superintendent; describes how to employ a well-designed process for board evaluation of superintendent performance as a relationship maintenance vehicle; and takes a close look at the very critical board chair-superintendent working relationship.

Chapter Two

Your Governing Lynchpin

The Board-Savvy Superintendent at Work

The Superintendent's Monthly Governance Coordinating Committee Meeting

The monthly work session of the superintendent and her senior administrative team sitting as the "governance coordinating committee" was winding down with a discussion of board-related issues that might need to be brought to the next meeting of the board's governance committee, which was responsible for overseeing the board's performance. The associate superintendent for curriculum and instruction, who served as "chief staff liaison" to the board's planning and development committee, suggested putting lagging attendance at committee meetings on the governance committee's agenda, and the chief financial officer, chief staff liaison to the board's performance monitoring committee, suggested that it might be a good idea if his committee chair run through the re-structured financial report with the governance committee so she'd be more comfortable presenting it at the full board meeting.

This fourth meeting of the superintendent's team wearing its governance coordinating committee hat had gone so well that the superintendent was convinced it'd been a great idea to dedicate a monthly meeting of her team to the governance function. They'd spent most of their time going over the agenda for the upcoming work session of the planning and development committee, which would be finalizing the operational planning/budget preparation calendar that the committee chair would be presenting at the next board meeting. Everyone agreed that the last item on the work session agen-

da should deal with the content of the slides the committee chair would be using, making sure he was comfortable with the presentation.

Rewarding the Board Chair with Nonmonetary Compensation

The superintendent was delighted to receive a letter from the chamber of commerce president inviting her to serve on the chamber's new business attraction and retention committee, which would be chaired by the CEO of the region's largest manufacturing firm and include other prominent business leaders as well as a number of elected officials and nonprofit CEOs. The superintendent had labored mightily to raise the profile of her district in the business community, including securing a seat on the chamber board a year after the district became a chamber member and paying her dues by faithfully attending every chamber board meeting and actively participating in the chamber subcommittee on business-education collaboration, which she had chaired for the past six months.. She felt honored to be asked to join this new heavyweight committee; not only would the work be fascinating, she'd also be rubbing elbows with the crème de la crème of the business community.

But rather than putting together her acceptance letter, she picked up the phone and called her board chair to see if he'd be interested in representing the district on this prestigious new chamber committee. She knew what his answer would be, since over the course of their weekly breakfast meetings he'd mentioned on several occasions his keen interest in economic development issues and his conviction that, as a successful entrepreneur who'd started two profitable business enterprises, he could make a real contribution to the community's development, economically speaking. She also knew he'd really appreciate her tossing the opportunity his way and that their working relationship couldn't help but grow even stronger as a result. And, from a personal perspective, she was pleased to be able to provide her chair with some well-earned nonmonetary compensation, since his enthusiastic backing made the difference a few months ago when she asked the board to approve hiring a new deputy superintendent for community relations. By the way, she was well aware he'd do a great job on the new committee, and that the district would be well-represented.

Nothing like Succeeding In Public

The new chair of the board's performance monitoring committee was ecstatic. "I told you you'd do great, despite your reservations" the superintendent said, when the chair stopped by his office after the board meeting to thank him for encouraging and supporting her in getting ready to present the committee's new financial report to the board. When the board had agreed to the new committee structure a year ago, they'd also adopted a set of commit-

tee guidelines that, among other things, provided that committee chairs and members would present reports at full board meetings, rather than the traditional approach of having all reports made by the superintendent and his top administrators. The performance monitoring committee, working closely with the superintendent and chief financial officer, had come up with a much more effective financial report over the course of two very intensive work sessions. Although all of the detail that'd gone to the board for years would still be provided as backup, the new report would employ bar charts and PowerPoint slides to educate board members on actual versus budget expenditures in major cost categories.

The superintendent knew that the report would be a real hit with the board, which had complained countless times about how hard it was to make sense of the bloated document they'd been receiving, whose pages and pages of numbers defied understanding. If there was ever a case of the trees burying the forest, this was it. However, he hadn't counted on the committee chair's crisis of confidence. Two weeks before the board meeting, she informed the superintendent over lunch that she couldn't possibly present the new report, explaining that as a housewife who'd never held a management position, she was really uncomfortable dealing with financial matters and was afraid she'd make a fool of herself trying to answer board members' questions. Her proposed solution: Open the presentation and immediately turn it over to the chief financial officer to go through the report and answer questions. It would have been easy for the superintendent to acquiesce; he certainly felt sympathetic. However, allowing the committee chair to give in to her fears would come at a high cost, in terms of both lost satisfaction and diminished ownership. So he took a stand, telling the chair that she "without question could do it, and do it very well," and that he'd make sure she was ready. Joined by the CFO, they met all morning the following Saturday, going through the financial report and discussing the answers to questions that might come up. They also held a full-fledged "dress rehearsal," having the chair stand up with the remote in hand and do a real-life run-through—twice. With myriad other pressing matters to attend to, it wasn't easy for the superintendent to spend so much time coaching, but he well knew that helping one of his key stakeholders on the board—the chair of a very important committee—succeed in public would pay a handsome dividend in terms of a more solid working relationship.

THE GOVERNING LYNCHPIN

Behind every school board doing a solid job of making high-impact governing judgments and decisions—and consequently making a real difference in district affairs—is a superintendent who is what I call "board-savvy." The board-savvy superintendent is not only an integral part of a district's Strategic Governing Team—along with board and executive team members—she is the lynchpin of the governing function. Actually, if she believes in strong governance, the superintendent has no choice but to play this critical role. After all, the great majority of board members are part-time, unpaid volunteers who typically have neither the governing expertise nor the time to develop and manage the school board as a governing body. As I pointed out in Chapter 1, many if not most school board members, in my experience, arrive at the district boardroom with only the vaguest notion of what governing work is all about. And since virtually all school boards are elected, rather than self-appointed like most nonprofit boards, board members tend not to have a strong incentive to develop themselves into a cohesive governing team, feeling more accountability to electors than their board teammates.

I didn't dream up the fictional scenarios that opened this chapter. Based on years of real-life experience, they capture the essence of the board-savvy superintendent, highlighting three preeminent characteristics that this chapter will explore in detail. The truly board-savvy superintendent:

1. *Brings a tremendously positive and collaborative attitude to her work with the school board.* She sees the board as one of her district's most precious assets, which she is accountable for developing and deploying on behalf of her district, and she sees herself as the board's preeminent governing partner.
2. *Makes the governing function a top chief executive priority.* He makes a real effort to become a true governing expert, knowing the field inside-out, and devotes significant time and attention to governing matters.
3. *Pays close attention of the human dimension of her working relationship with her board.* She is dedicated to transforming board members into satisfied owners of their governing work, and she pays close attention to building and maintaining rock-solid working relationships with her preeminent stakeholders on the board—the board chair and the chairs of the board's standing committees.

POTHOLES ON THE ROAD TO BOARD SAVVY-NESS

Any superintendent can become more board-savvy if he is committed to effective governance and to playing a leading role on the district's Strategic Governing Team. And experience has taught that superintendents who are by nature extroverts with a strong collaborative streak will have an easier time building their board savvy-ness. However, on the road to board savvy-ness you might have to contend with some formidable barriers. One is the lack of formal academic preparation. A couple of weeks ago, keynoting a conference of superintendents from all over Colorado, I asked how many in the audience had had a really thorough course in graduate school on building a close, positive, and productive working relationship with their board—a question I've asked umpteen times over the years, at AASA and NSBA meetings and in workshops. Of the 120-some superintendents, only a handful—perhaps seven or eight—raised their hand. I wasn't in the least surprised, since the response was depressingly typical. Despite the obvious influence school boards wield in district affairs—including hiring and firing the superintendent, adopting the annual operating plan and budget, setting strategic directions, and fashioning district-wide policies, among other things—and their impact on the superintendent's professional success, superintendent-aspirants are still much more likely to learn about the ins and outs of curriculum planning than the much more CEO-like governing functions.

Another barrier superintendent-aspirants are likely to encounter is the absence of on-the-job governance training as they climb the professional ladder in their district. Not only is direct interaction with board members highly unlikely before reaching the senior administrative level (especially in the absence of board standing committees), even then interaction is likely to be highly formal, limited to the monthly board meeting, and the great majority of executive teams I've observed over the years tend not to make board operations a major ongoing agenda item. In practice, this means that many newly minted superintendents, not coming to the top job well-armed with practical governing wisdom, are highly vulnerable. Interviewing new superintendents over the years, I've been astounded at how ill-equipped new superintendents often are to build solid working relationships with their boards. To take a recent example, when I asked a new superintendent I was interviewing if she'd given much thought to ways she could transform her board members into satisfied owners of their strategic planning work, the response was a blank stare. "What do you mean by owners?" she responded, saying that she saw her job as basically getting board members the information they needed to make sound decisions. End of story! Being highly intelligent, she didn't have any trouble, as we talked, understanding why board members' feelings of ownership could be fostered by active involvement and were critical to their commitment. However, I was, not for the first time by far, appalled that we'd even had to have the discussion.

And there is another powerful barrier to becoming board-savvy that I think of as cultural since it tends to be absorbed as one moves up the K–12 career ladder: the defensive we/they syndrome. Trapped by this very common view of the governing arena, un-board-savvy superintendents tend to see the governing work of the board as fundamentally different from the executive and administrative work of the superintendent and her top lieutenants—separated from each other by a solid dividing line that can't be safely crossed. This essentially static—and totally unrealistic view—is a major impediment to creative board-superintendent-executive team collaboration in getting governing decisions and judgments made. Rather than seeing complex governing decisions (for example, adopting a new vision statement or set of strategic goals) as the product of intensive creative collaboration of both board and staff members, this view often results in a kind of rule-making approach that is preoccupied with distinguishing between the board's "policy making" role and the superintendent's and executive team's executive role, focusing on what the board shouldn't do, rather than what it should be doing to make more effective governing decisions. The we/they syndrome also has another negative aspect that impedes partnership building: seeing the board as essentially a damage control challenge, often in terms of guarding against the horrors of board "micro-management." It's extremely difficult, in my experience, for a superintendent to come up with creative ways to involve board members in shaping important governing decisions so they feel ownership and hence commitment to those decisions, when the superintendent is preoccupied with protecting herself from board incursions into executive territory. Fear and defensiveness are, indeed, the preeminent enemies of board-superintendent partnership building.

A POSITIVE AND COLLABORATIVE ATTITUDE

"I'm blessed with a group that's got the makings of a really effective board." As soon as the new superintendent of a mid-size Midwestern district said this in our first meeting in response to my request to describe his board, I figured I'd be working with a board-savvy chief executive, and I was right. Looking back on that experience, I'm positive that his success in building a rock-solid partnership with his board during his first year on the job had a lot to do with his attitude. During that first meeting, he proceeded to run down the roster of board members, pointing out what he thought each one could uniquely contribute to the governing task ahead, for example: the retired former teacher who cared deeply about students and could bring years of experience to bear on addressing student achievement issues; the business owner whose grasp of financial matters would be a real asset in grappling with budgetary issues; the marketing executive who would understand the importance of reaching out to the community, communicating district priorities and accomplishments and paying attention to citizen concerns; the active community volunteer who served on a number of nonprofit boards and could help build ties to key community stakeholders.

It was immediately clear from what he said that, in his mind, his school board was a precious district asset, not merely a burden he had to contend with—that he saw the board in terms of its leadership potential rather than its shortcomings. This is one of the preeminent characteristics of the board-savvy chief executives I've worked with over the years. In common with other board-savvy chief executives, however, he didn't naively assume that his board's leadership promise would automatically be realized in practice. He not only knew that capitalizing on the board as an asset would involve systematically developing the board's governing capacity, he also recognized that it would be totally unrealistic to expect board members to take the lead in capacity building. So, as I'll discuss in detail in chapter 3, this board-savvy superintendent, wearing his "Chief Board Developer" hat, convinced his board president, and soon after the other board officers, to put together a governance task force to work with the superintendent and a governance consultant in coming up with practical ways to strengthen the board's governing role, structure, and processes.

A TOP CHIEF EXECUTIVE PRIORITY

Sitting in on a special work session of a school board's strategic and operational planning committee a year ago gave me a valuable opportunity to see a truly board-savvy superintendent at work. The sole agenda item was to map out the key steps required to update the district's long-range strategic plan, which clearly fell within the committee's bailiwick. By the way, since the board was quite small—only five members—dividing board members into committees didn't make sense. So strategic and operational planning was what you might call a "virtual" committee: all board members meeting as a committee of the whole, wearing the planning hat, under the leadership of a board member who'd been appointed chair. The other virtual committee—performance oversight and external relations—was headed by a different board member when the whole board met wearing this hat. The beauty of this half-loaf approach was that it focused the board's attention on each of two key governing areas without mixing them together.

The superintendent played a major but untraditional role in this planning process design session. Rather than bringing a finished planning process document to the committee and asking board members to thumb through it, he instead opened the session with a presentation on major trends in the field of strategic planning, introducing an approach that was new to all but one of the board members: running two planning streams concurrently—one aimed at fashioning "out of the box" change initiatives to address issues that didn't fit within the district's current programmatic/functional structure (for example, the pressing need to re-build community confidence in the school system), and the other aimed at updating long-range goals for existing functions. I'll discuss board involvement in the planning function in detail in chapter 4, but this brief example illustrates a board-savvy superintendent at work who truly does make governing a top chief executive priority, by making the effort to become a world class expert in key governing functions, such as strategic planning and change management. A less-savvy superintendent might have convinced the board to get caught up in the kind of monster comprehensive long-range planning processes that used to be quite popular, but have proved to be a bust in terms of dealing with critical issues. A tremendous amount of board and staff time would have been wasted creating a huge planning tome that ultimately sat on the shelf.

Becoming a true expert in a field as complex and rapidly developing as nonprofit and public governance is no mean feat, in light of the myriad pressing demands on all chief executives, but board-savvy CEOs know that they've got no choice; otherwise, their boards could all too easily miss opportunities to provide high-impact leadership or get embroiled in counterproductive activities that actually erode their governing performance and consequently weaken the board-superintendent partnership (keep in mind that board members who don't feel productive and satisfied tend to be unreliable partners for the chief executive). To take another example, board members in diverse nonprofit/public sectors, such as aging, transportation, and K–12 education, have in recent years become actively involved in the external relations area, often by being booked to speak in key external forums such as chamber of commerce and Rotary luncheons, and this involvement has been well-documented in the governance literature. Such involvement has proved to yield a rich return on the investment of board member time, in terms of stronger relationships with key stakeholder organizations and enhanced board member satisfaction. Only a truly board-savvy superintendent who takes the trouble to read widely in the governance field and avidly pursues other educational opportunities, such as attending governance workshops, will be up-to-date on important developments in this rapidly changing field.

Making governance a top-tier chief executive priority involves more than a board-savvy superintendent's acquiring knowledge and expertise in the field. It also means devoting substantial time and attention to the board's functioning as a governing organization—paying close attention to the nuts and bolts mechanics of governing. You'll recall that in chapter 1 I described the school board as, by definition, an organization: a formally constituted group of people working closely together, within a formal policy framework, in carrying out a specific mission: to govern. Of course, school boards aren't just *any* organization; they're unique in at least four major respects. First, they wield tremendous power and influence through their governing decisions and judgments, including hiring and firing the superintendent, adopting the annual operating plan and budget, setting strategic targets, funding major change initiatives, establishing district-wide operating policies, and approving new positions in the table of organization, among other things. Second, their governing work is extraordinarily complex and far less well understood than such staples of K–12 leadership and management as curriculum and instructional development or building management. Third, consisting for the most part of part-time volunteers who often have only the haziest notion of what governing is all about, school boards have slight in-built self-management capability, unlike every other organization making up the modern school district. And fourth, because school board members are for the most part elected, melding them into a cohesive governing team that operates according to shared norms is a daunting challenge, to say the least.

The picture I've painted isn't a rosy one, as superintendents well know; an undermanaged board can easily get out of control, doing considerable damage to the educational enterprise. I saw this happen, much to my dismay, three or so years ago, when a stunningly un-board-savvy superintendent passively watched two renegade board members hijack his school board, impeach his performance, and convince a majority to vote for his dismissal. His aloofness from the fray meant that there was no counter-force working to keep the board on an even keel as a governing body. What keeps the board on-course, more than any other factor in my experience, is a board-savvy superintendent who embraces management of the governing function and the board's nuts and bolts operations as a top chief executive priority. I've written and spoken widely about a very simple but powerful approach to fulfilling this chief executive management function that many superintendents have successfully employed: serving as the CEO not only of all district operations, but also of a very special "governing program" called board operations. Of course, the board-savvy superintendent plays this critical role largely behind the scenes, and she knows enough never to drop even a hint to the board that she is its chief executive officer.

At the individual level, several board-savvy superintendents I know make a point of devoting a couple of hours every weekend to thinking about board operations, identifying what appear to be developing issues and strategizing how to work with their board in addressing them. For example, one of these superintendents pinpointed a potentially serious issue relating to the board's performance oversight and monitoring committee: a committee chair who was turning out to be a weak leader, partly because of his laid-back style and partly because of his lack of confidence in dealing with financial matters, combined with a new, very aggressive committee member, a financial virtuoso who was increasingly assuming the de facto chair role. She understood that allowing the chair to fail would come at a high price, in terms of a humiliated board member who had been convinced to assume an important role and then left foundering.

Her strategy? Spend an hour with the board chair, discussing how to buttress the committee chair, via hands-on counseling and a concerted effort to prepare the chair to lead committee meetings. She and her board chair also agreed to appoint the aggressive new committee member to chair a newly established task force to explore revenue diversification possibilities, working under the mother performance oversight and monitoring committee. Their assumption, which proved accurate, was that keeping the challenging new committee member busy in an ego satisfying role would give the chair time to grow in the role. This is what I mean by nuts and bolts attention to board operations.

More formally and visibly, many board-savvy superintendents work closely with the board committee responsible for oversight of board operations, often called "governance" or "board operations." Seeing themselves as both members of, and chief staff to, the committee, these board-savvy superintendents make sure that the committee is carrying out its responsibility. To take a recent real-life example, well into its second year of operation, the governance committee of a school board had not yet tackled one of its primary responsibilities: to fashion a set of individual board member "governing targets and guidelines" that could be used both to orient newly elected board members and to monitor board members' performance. One reason nothing had yet been accomplished, it appeared to the superintendent, was a normal reluctance among board members to appear to be evaluating each other's performance, but failing to take advantage of this opportunity to strengthen the board's self-management capacity, if only modestly, would exact a high price in the superintendent's opinion.

So rather than sit back, she took the initiative: developing the outline of a simple, straightforward process for coming up with targets and guidelines and for ongoing monitoring and reviewing it with the chair, who would, she recommended, run it by the governance committee. As it played out, the governance committee hosted a special half-day session of the whole board, at which targets and guidelines were brainstormed (for example, that board members would attend all full board and committee meetings; that they would come to meetings well-prepared; that they would follow a particular process for arranging to visit buildings; that they could not request information from senior administrators reporting to the superintendent that would require more than a half-hour to compile; and the like). This board-savvy superintendent also suggested how the board chair might lead the governance committee through the process of fine-tuning and finalizing the targets and guidelines and she proposed a simple monitoring process that the chair could review with the committee.

Wearing the board program CEO hat, many superintendents have made the members of their senior administrative team part of the governance management process, as I pointed out earlier in this chapter, by engaging them in formal governance management structure and process. One way that this has worked well is for the superintendent to designate particular members of the team to be the lead person (sometimes called the "chief staff liaison") for particular board standing committees, such as planning and monitoring (either actual committees or the whole board meeting as a "virtual" committee). These lead staff are typically accountable for developing agendas for upcoming committee meetings and reviewing them with the superintendent's top lieutenants, meeting as what is often called the "governance coordinating committee." Armed with input from executive colleagues, the liaisons then typically revise the agenda, which they then review with their committee chairs, making sure that the chairs are well-prepared to lead committee deliberations.

Board-savvy superintendents wearing their board program CEO hat are alert to the need for direct involvement in the process I've just described, beyond chairing the monthly governance coordinating committee meetings. For example, when a prominent business executive newly elected to the school board agreed to chair the board's recently established community relations committee, the superintendent, thinking that it was critical to get this new committee off to a good start and to ensure that the new chair was an unqualified success in his role as the committee's leader, invited the committee chair and the staff liaison to join her for a 90-minute meeting in her office, where, over lunch, they would discuss the committee's responsibilities and the chair's role in detail, and also map out some specific committee targets over the coming year.

For example, in the committee's functional description that the board had adopted by resolution was the responsibility to oversee the development and implementation of strategies to promote a positive district image in the community and among critical stakeholders, such as the board of county commissioners and city council. Discussing this responsibility in her office, the superintendent, committee chair, and staff liaison agreed that the sensible first step would be for the committee to meet in a special work session to fashion a set of "image elements," consisting of the key messages that needed to be communicated to the wider community, which would guide staff in fashioning image-building strategies for committee review. Before adjourning, they also mapped out a methodology that the committee might follow in developing the image elements.

Playing a hands-on role as CEO of her district's board program is obviously a time-consuming responsibility. How much time? Experience has taught that board-savvy superintendents spend somewhere between 25 and 30 percent of their time in the role. To devote less than 25 percent to board operations would be a dangerous strategy to pursue, risking not only board underperformance and dysfunction as a governing body, but also jeopardizing the board-superintendent partnership.

TURNING BOARD MEMBERS INTO SATISFIED OWNERS

Everyone was tired but satisfied at the end of their day together. The "strategic work session," which involved the board, superintendent, and top administrators, had gotten the annual strategic planning cycle off to a great start:

- *Planning committee members had set the stage with their opening presentation on environmental conditions and trends affecting the district, such as the influx of Spanish-speaking students and the continued decline of households with children in the schools.*
- *Nine breakout groups led by board members—meeting in three rounds over the course of the day—generated a tremendous amount of content: preliminary values and vision statements; the identification of issues related to evolving student needs, technology, district finances, the district's external relationships, and governance, and the exploration of possible change initiatives.*
- *The follow-through process had been affirmed, including the role of the planning committee in coordinating follow-through steps.*

That evening, looking back on the day, the superintendent recognized that she and the consultant retained to facilitate the session had made the right call when they convinced planning committee members to open the session with a well-rehearsed conditions/trends presentation and to make board member-led breakout groups a centerpiece of the session. Although at times it'd seemed like a three-ring circus, there was no question that active board member leadership and engagement played a key role in achieving the session's two principal goals: generating high-quality planning content that could be put to good use in fashioning strategic directions and change initiatives in the coming months; and transforming board members into strong owners of the strategic planning process who could be depended on to provide strong support in following through on the work session.

This fictional scenario, which draws on years of real-life experience, illustrates how well-designed processes for actively and meaningfully engaging board members early enough to make a significant difference is a tried and true way to transform them into satisfied owners of their governing work. This is a top priority for board-savvy superintendents, who are keenly aware that board members who are strong owners of their governing work make for more reliable partners, primarily because ownership fuels the kind of board commitment that superintendents can depend on in carrying out governing decisions (such as adopting a new vision statement to guide district planning). Therefore, as I'll discuss in detail in chapter 4, wearing their "Chief Process Designer" hat, board-savvy superintendents devote a lot of time and attention to designing processes that will foster board ownership. A less board-savvy superintendent might have taken a more traditional approach to strategic planning less attuned to the human dimension of the board-superintendent working relationship, such as merely retaining a consulting firm to put together a strategic plan and run it by the board. Of course, shelves are filled with such plans that have gone unimplemented because un-board-savvy superintendents have failed to recognize that audiences for finished staff work don't make for committed owners.

Board-savvy superintendents know that board member satisfaction buttresses the commitment that ownership breeds. Although the fundamental path to deep board member satisfaction is engagement in doing important governing work that makes a significant difference in a school district's affairs (such as a major uptick in student achievement), board-savvy superintendents know that regularly meeting board members' ego needs and finding ways to make their governing work more enjoyable are important ways to enhance satisfaction. One reason that board-led breakout groups have become a staple of strategic work sessions like the one described above is that they not only generate substantial content, but also provide breakout group leaders with an ego-satisfying experience. Likewise, having board standing committee chairs present committee reports at full board meetings, rather than relying on staff to do all the reporting, serves the same human purpose, and building the regular rotation of chairs into a board's committee guidelines is a tried and true way of spreading ego satisfaction more widely.

A cautionary note regarding the use of breakout groups and standing committees to promote ego satisfaction is in order. Whenever a board member is asked to play a public role in a work session or board meeting, board-savvy superintendents know that they've got to make sure the board member succeeds. They're keenly aware that there's no surer way of turning a board member into an adversary than asking her to accept a responsibility and then allowing her to fail publicly. This is why a board-savvy superintendent I worked with recently insisted that the board members who would be leading breakout groups in an upcoming planning retreat receive a thorough orientation on the ins and outs of breakout group facilitation and on the specific tasks that each breakout group was being asked to perform in the retreat (such as identifying and assessing financial issues). This is also why board-savvy superintendents go out of their way to help standing committee chairs succeed in leading their committees and in presenting committee reports to the board. As a really board-savvy superintendent commented recently about her committee chairs, "I make sure I care enough to help them do their very best, and that I'll never let them down."

We've looked at major ways to foster board members' feelings of ownership and satisfaction, but board-savvy superintendents also pay close attention to the finer human touches that have a powerful cumulative effect over time, such as making sure that board members are publicly recognized in district publications and the external media and adding spice to the governing process by, for example, rotating board meeting locations among district buildings and building a segment into the board agenda to showcase innovative programs.

FOR BOARD MEMBERS: HIRING A BOARD-SAVVY SUPERINTENDENT

The more board-savvy the superintendent, the more effective the board is likely to be as a governing body and the more favorable the odds of building a rock-solid board-superintendent partnership that can withstand the inevitable stresses and strains that come with leading a modern school system. So school boards have a big stake in recruiting superintendents whose governing intelligence is well developed, but, sad to say, many recruitment efforts I've observed have paid scant attention to the board savvy-ness of candidates. I'll close, therefore, with some practical tips for determining how board-savvy particular candidates are:

> Your search committee should interview at least the officers of the candidate's current or immediate past board, asking them to assess the board's working relationship with the candidate in terms of strengths and weakness, to identify important relationship issues that might have developed, and to describe how particular issues were resolved (or not).
>
> Your search committee should also directly ask the candidate probing, open-ended questions aimed at determining his or her board savvy-ness in terms of governing knowledge, philosophy, and methodology, for example:

- What is your detailed definition of the governing role and major functions of the school board?
- How would you assess your working relationship with your current (or immediate past) board in terms of: strengths and weaknesses; relationship issues; how issues were resolved?
- What concrete steps did you take to help your board become a more effective governing body?
- What concrete steps did you take to strengthen your working relationship with your board?
- What steps did you take to help your current (or immediate past) board play a more effective role in district planning and performance monitoring?
- What board committees have you worked with and which ones were most effective in promoting effective board governing performance?
- What do you consider the key elements of an effective process for our board to evaluate your performance?

Of course, there are many other questions you might ask, but the point is to be both specific and open-ended in asking about a candidate's governing knowledge, philosophy, and experience. In my experience, it doesn't take very long, if you listen carefully, to get a good sense of a candidate's board savvy-ness.

Chapter Three

Designing Your Board as a Governing Body

INHERIT OR DESIGN?

In chapter 1 I pointed out that a school board is by definition an organization within the school district's overall organizational structure: a formally constituted group of people working together, within a framework of policies, in carrying out a common mission—to govern the school district. Therefore, a school board isn't essentially different from any other organization within your district structure, such as the office of the superintendent or the department of curriculum and instruction. However, your school board is without question a very special kind of organization—consisting of elected volunteers in the great majority of cases, wielding more formal power than any other organization within your district structure, setting district-wide directions, and dealing regularly with the most complex, highest-stakes issues facing your district. That said, it's important to keep in mind that the school board is like all the other organizations making up your district structure in a very important respect: it can be consciously, explicitly developed—or designed—in order to enhance its capacity to carry out its mission.

In practice, this means that the Strategic Governing Team of your district—its board, superintendent, and senior executives—has a clear choice to make: merely inherit the board of yesterday or consciously design the board of today and the future. This chapter takes a detailed look at the school board development—or design—process, which involves developing what you might think of as the architecture of the board: the people serving on the board; the board's governing role; and the board's governing structure. There is a compelling reason to deal with the board design process in this book on building a high-impact board-superintendent Strategic Governing Team.

33

Boards that are explicitly designed, rather than merely inherited, tend to do a more effective job of making governing decisions and judgments, thereby providing board members with greater satisfaction and, hence, making them more reliable governing partners with the superintendent. Board-savvy superintendents, well knowing that a well-developed governing body makes for a better governing partner, are always ardent advocates for systemic board development who take the lead in the design process.

MAJOR BOARD DESIGN VERSUS ONGOING TWEAKING

A few weeks ago, I talked with the board president and superintendent of a large suburban district in the Southeast, who described their governance situation, making the following points:

- There was a high degree of frustration among board members, the majority of whom were quite vocal about not feeling certain about their detailed governing role and not believing that they were in the driver's seat in terms of making high-stakes governing decisions. The board president made the point that several board members had told her they'd become extremely frustrated by serving as a passive audience for largely-finished staff work.
- Board meetings tended to run into the wee hours with lots of staff show-and-tell reports and often-heated debate, and only rare consensus on what appeared to be the highest-priority issues, which tended to remain on the board's agenda meeting after meeting. Tempers were often frayed and discourse distinctly un-civil. A cohesive governing team this board definitely wasn't.
- The board was saddled with a structure of narrowly defined standing committees having more to do with administrative functions and program details than with the work of governing—for example, finance, curriculum and instruction, personnel, buildings and grounds, and similar committees. Because the board consisted of only seven members, every board member served on at least 3 committees, so their precious time was being chopped up into small bites. As the board president described it, board members felt more like "technical advisers" than high-level governors.
- The school board hadn't within the past decade taken a close look at its governing performance or at its governing role, structure, and processes; nor was there a formal governing improvement strategy or plan of any kind.
- An increasingly unhappy board meant that the board-superintendent partnership was deteriorating and appeared to be in serious jeopardy.

"What's your diagnosis?" they asked me. My response was that it sounded like this district's governing structure badly needed a complete overhaul, dealing with the governing knowledge and skills of board members, the board's overall governing role, and the board's governing structure. This was clearly a situation calling for fundamental governing re-design; merely tweaking this or that element of the board's governing architecture wouldn't suffice. This chapter is about that kind of comprehensive, in-depth governing design process. In chapter 4, I deal with what I think of as continuous governing improvement: employing well-designed standing committees that work closely with the superintendent and her top lieutenants in tweaking the board's engagement in such key governing areas as strategic and operational planning and performance monitoring. Keep in mind that once a major design effort has taken place, and the board's role and structure have been thoroughly updated, annual tweaking of processes should suffice for several years.

A RIGHT WAY AND A WRONG WAY

The Strategic Governing Team of District A has put together a "high-impact governing" task force consisting of three board members and the superintendent that has been charged to come up with concrete recommendations for strengthening the board's governing capacity and the board-superintendent partnership. With the assistance of a governance consultant, the task force will over the course of six work sessions in the next four months identify critical governance issues and put together a detailed game plan for updating the board's role and structure, which task force members will present to the full board in a special work session. The superintendent of District B, having little patience with elaborate process, has talked his school board into taking a more direct approach to board development that will consume much less board member time. A consulting firm has been retained to study the board's governing structure and processes and to come up with an action report recommending steps that should be taken to strengthen the board's governing capacity and the board-superintendent working relationship. The District B approach can be completed in only two months.

Which approach is most likely to result in the actual implementation of governance improvements? Group A's, of course, for the obvious reason that the active involvement of three board members in shaping the governance improvement recommendations will transform the three board members into what I call "change champions"—owners who will take the lead in convincing their peers on the board to act on the recommendations. Experience has taught that the ownership that comes from active board engagement is a critical element in successfully implementing change on the governance front. As a consultant, I learned this valuable lesson the painful way early in my career, in the school of hard knocks. I'll never forget standing at the podium before a nine-person school board a couple of decades ago—splendid in my pin-stripe consultant suit with my heavily starched shirt and power tie—drawing on my research and expertise in telling board members what they needed to do to become a more effective governing body. They weren't hostile, just coldly polite, as I walked through the recommendations in my report, and I could tell from the questions that they weren't buying much of what I was selling. As it turned out, some useful tweaks resulted from my report—for example, upgrading the process for orienting new board members and formalizing a process for board evaluation of the superintendent—but the centerpiece of my report—a new standing committee structure—never stood a chance. The superintendent thought the report made sense, and so did the board president, but neither was inclined to go to the ramparts for deeper change.

NEVER UNDERESTIMATE RESISTANCE

Resistance to change has scuttled more than one change ship in the sea of K–12 governance; in fact, it makes sense to assume that whatever approach your district takes to fundamental board design, you'll have to overcome inevitable—and often formidable—resistance, which is why transforming board members into owners of change is so critical. Resistance is often the result of an unfortunate experience with a poorly conceived and executed change process. For example, when I was interviewing school board members in preparation for a strategic planning retreat a few years ago, three trustees made a point of warning me not to go down a particular path if I wanted to accomplish anything as their consultant. They were referring to a dismal Saturday the board had spent a couple of years earlier that they considered a monumental waste of their time and energy—and, as far as they were concerned, a grievous insult to the board. The board members had been led through a "team building" process in a retreat setting that involved them in some classic "touchy-feely" exercises intended to promote more honest communication, lower emotional barriers, and foster a spirit of collaboration. As is often the case with such therapeutic approaches, the warm glow they'd generated wore off quickly when the inevitable Monday came, and participants encountered a fundamentally unchanged organizational structure. Confusing cosmetic with fundamental organizational change is a sure-fire recipe for frustration and often disillusionment.

And even without a sour experience to draw on, many, if not most, board members I've worked with over the years instinctively resist important change because of fear—that comfortable (if not particularly satisfying) routines will be disrupted, that influence will be lost, that much more time and effort will be demanded, that there is the possibility of publicly failing at playing a new role and suffering the consequent embarrassment. At a recent governance workshop I conducted for superintendents, one of the participants told an on-point true story. One of the most ardent critics of the new committee structure that the board of this superintendent's district was considering—as part of a comprehensive set of recommendations put together by a board task force—was a long-tenured board member who had chaired the board's finance committee for the past ten years—long enough to be described in a district newsletter as "Mr. Finance." Already a financial whizz who headed his own CPA firm, he'd become a true expert in the district's finances, and what gave him particular satisfaction was working closely with the district's chief financial officer in putting together the annual budget and recommending it to the board. The master of every financial nook and cranny, he led the committee with a sure hand in going through the budget line-items.

The rub came from the task force's recommendation to fold the existing finance committee into the new, more broad-based performance oversight and monitoring committee, whose functions included monitoring district financial performance, and—adding insult to injury in this long-time board veteran's eyes—the transfer of the budget preparation function to the new planning and development committee. Conversations with both the board president and superintendent made clear that the loss of stature and influence was a huge issue to this board member, along with sacrificing the ego satisfaction that came with chairing the finance committee. In retrospect, it would have made sense to involve this obstreperous critic in the task force that had come up with the recommendations, but the second-best solution did the trick: the board president's appointing this long-time board member the first chair of the new planning and development committee.

Fear of failing probably equals potential loss of influence as a barrier to governance change. Another true story I heard in my recent governance workshop came from a superintendent whose board's governance task force had strongly recommended that board members be actively engaged in speaking on behalf of their district in important public forums, as part of a "board speakers bureau" coordinated by the board's new community/stakeholder relations committee. This seemingly minor recommendation was vociferously opposed by one of the newer board members, who forced participants in the governance work session to devote a precious half-hour to discussing the pros and cons of a speakers' bureau. Only later, over a drink with the board members, did the superintendent realize that at the heart of her trustee's resistance was visceral fear of public speaking, something she's avoided like the plague for years. The public explanation of her resistance—

the time required to represent the district in various forums—turned out to be a minor concern.

THE PREEMINENT GOVERNANCE CHANGE CHAMPIONS

I was fortunate a couple of years ago to sit in on a fascinating special board work session at which the school board president and superintendent teamed up to make a powerful case for a daylong governance retreat involving all board members and the superintendent's top lieutenants. With the aid of a professional facilitator, they explained, the retreat would focus on exploring issues related to the board's role, structure, and processes and brainstorming possible solutions, and the facilitator would follow-up by developing a formal set of recommendations for board review six weeks or so after the retreat. Two things struck me forcefully as I observed the session. First, the board president took the lead in presenting and explaining the retreat recommendations. The superintendent played a backup role, answering occasional questions but not making any of the formal presentation. Second, the board president was obviously anything but a figurehead. He was clearly highly knowledgeable about advances in the field of K–12 governance and had given serious thought to the board's performance as a governing body. He certainly got everyone's attention at the very beginning by pointing out that in his opinion the board was "falling really short of its leadership potential" and dangerously close to becoming a "dysfunctional" governing body. Not only was he a passionate and well-informed advocate for the retreat, he'd also taken the trouble to become completely comfortable with the Power-Point slides he used to illustrate his points, evincing none of the awkwardness resulting from an under-rehearsed presentation that can seriously reduce a presenter's impact.

From the comments of three or four board members I chatted with after the work session, it was clear that the board president's advocacy had sealed the deal, and I'm confident that if the superintendent had gone it alone, or had taken the lead, with the president playing a subordinate role, the odds of getting the board to commit to a full day would have been far less likely. I later learned from the very board-savvy superintendent who had backed up her board president in the work session that getting the president to take the lead hadn't been a piece of cake. Indeed, it was the result of a carefully conceived strategy that had played out over the period of five months or so. A brilliant entrepreneur who'd built a highly successful software company, the board president had been little interested in the ins and outs of governing when he joined the board two years earlier; his passion was student achievement, and he intended to hold the superintendent's—and her executives'—feet to the fire on the issue. And when after his first year on the school board, he'd been elected president, he had made clear to the superintendent that, while he would do his best to lead orderly and productive board meetings, he had neither the time nor the interest to get involved in the nuts and bolts of governing.

So the board-savvy superintendent had her work cut out for her over the coming five months if she wanted her new president to take the lead in spearheading a concerted board development effort. Her commitment to the task of transforming her president into an effective advocate wasn't solely the result an altruistic belief in strong board leadership; she also recognized that allowing her board to continue to under-perform for much longer and consequently to grow more frustrated, would very likely erode her partnership with the board and might even jeopardize her position as CEO. She began her stealth campaign with a low-keyed educational strategy over a period of two months or so, sharing a couple of books and several articles on school governance with her chair and making a point of discussing them over a series of breakfasts. They also drove together to a governance workshop sponsored by the state school board association, spending a couple of hours discussing governance issues each way.

The foundation now laid, the superintendent's next step in transforming her president into an owner of, and advocate for, board capacity building took her into ego territory. In a nutshell, over another series of breakfast meetings she convinced her president that the most powerful possible imprint of his leadership, and the most enduring legacy he could leave, would be a fully developed board that was capable of governing at a high level. Over and over again, she hammered home the point that student achievement wasn't just a matter of what happened in the classroom; it was also dependent on decisions made in the boardroom—about district strategic goals, educational strategies, and budget allocations. She also made sure her president understood that building the board's governing capacity by updating its role and structure couldn't be accomplished by simply putting the board through some kind of training program or by the superintendent merely telling the board what it needed to do to become more effective. With her president now firmly bought into the idea of spearheading the board development effort, the two of them met with the board secretary and treasurer to share their thinking about board development and ask for their support of the retreat recommendation at the upcoming special board work session that had been scheduled. These other two board officers weren't asked to share in the presentation— that would have been unrealistic—but to be vocally supportive during the discussion. They were, and it almost certainly made a difference.

The final step in this board-savvy superintendent's strategy was to make 100 percent sure the president was a smash hit as the lead presenter at the special board work session—ensuring that he would be a stellar presenter and make a compelling case for holding the daylong governance retreat. Al-

though this might sound like a finer touch—a kind of cherry on the sundae—
it was actually a critical step in the process. The superintendent was board-
savvy enough to understand two things: first, a powerful presentation by her
president would be essential to overcoming inevitable resistance from two
influential board veterans; and second, if the president stumbled in the presentation, wounded pride and embarrassment would likely reduce, and perhaps even destroy, his commitment to board development. She also understood that business success and years as a CEO wouldn't guarantee success
at the podium, especially with a new set of slides. So she talked her president
into doing two real-life run-throughs of his presentation in her conference
room, becoming completely comfortable with the slides and responding to
questions from the superintendent. By the way, he later thanked her for
caring enough to make sure he did his very best.

TWO POWERFUL BOARD DESIGN VEHICLES

Before getting involved in a process aimed at fundamental re-design of your
district's governing board, it is imperative you ask two very important questions. First, is the process under consideration technically sound, in the sense
that it is capable of generating concrete governing improvements such as an
updated board governing role and committee structure? Second, is the process psychologically sound, in the sense that it will generate sufficient ownership among participants to fuel the commitment required for implementation? Hiring a consultant to put together design recommendations and present
them to the board, or depending on the superintendent to play this role, might
be technically sound, but would certainly fail the psychological test, in both
cases turning the board members into passive audience members rather than
committed owners. Two vehicles that have proved in practice to be technically and psychologically sound are the governance retreat and the governance
task force. Before turning to the substantive elements of the school board's
governing design, I'll take a brief look at each of these vehicles.

The retreat approach makes good sense if the intensive, front-end involvement of all board members is considered critical to the ultimate success
of the board design effort. Situations that call for a governance retreat include: a board characterized by a high level of distrust among board members and the absence of consensus on the board's governing role; a brand-
new board-superintendent relationship; and significant resistance among a
majority of board members to change on the governing front. The term
"retreat" is normally applied to a work session lasting at least a day, which is
typically held at a location other than the boardroom and which deals with
matters that cannot effectively be handled in a board business meeting. As
many readers well know, retreats can easily fall apart if not meticulously

planned and managed, leaving resentment and frustration in their wake. And since board members are involved failure almost always comes at a high cost, which the superintendent all too often bears. Districts that have brought off successful retreats, such as the Baltimore County Public Schools (Maryland) and the Chesterfield County Public Schools (Virginia) have ensured success by:

- *Employing an ad hoc retreat design committee.* Involving one-fourth to one-third of the board members, along with the superintendent, in an ad hoc committee that is responsible for designing the retreat, has proved to be an effective way to ensure the retreat's legitimacy in board members' eyes. Involving more than a third of the board in the committee is apt to be politically risky, since it makes the sting of exclusion much sharper. Making the design committee more diverse will enhance the retreat's legitimacy—for example, by including a new board member or even one who has been vocally skeptical of having a retreat. I can think of many examples of critics turning into supporters as a result of being involved in designing a retreat.
- *Developing a detailed design.* Making sure that the committee produces a comprehensive, detailed design for the retreat not only helps to ensure that the retreat will be successful, but also reduces resistance by making clear what will transpire during the day together. Participants who feel confident that their time will be productively spent are far more likely to look forward to the retreat than participants who are left in the dark. The detailed retreat design includes: the objectives to be achieved (for example, identifying and assessing governance issues; mapping out a preliminary board governing role); the structure of the retreat (where it will be held; the breakout groups that will be used); and the blow-by-blow agenda.
- *Involving executive team members.* It is advisable to involve all of the members of the superintendent's executive team (typically her direct reports) in the retreat, for three very important reasons. First, they bring valuable information to the table (for example, recent advances in the field of teaching English as a second language). Second, their involvement fosters a positive board-executive working relationship, primarily because board and executive team members get to know each other better through their breakout group work in the retreat. And third, their involvement better prepares them to support the implementation of board improvement steps resulting from the retreat, not only because of their understanding of the technical content of the steps, but also because of the ownership resulting from their involvement in shaping the improvement steps.
- *Making use of board-led breakout groups.* Breakout groups dealing with important topics (for example, mapping out the board's primary governing responsibilities; coming up with a list of board member performance tar-

gets) not only generate important content that can be used in following through on the retreat, they are also a reliable vehicle for actively engaging participants. Having board members lead the groups is a sure-fire way to strengthen board ownership of the retreat and to provide board members with ego satisfaction. However, once board members have agreed to lead particular groups, the superintendent must ensure that they succeed in the role; stumbling and suffering embarrassment are guaranteed to reduce commitment to following through on the retreat. Success can be assured by defining the work each group is responsible for accomplishing in detail and making sure the leader is provided with a thorough orientation on both the breakout group's responsibilities and guidelines for leading the group (for example, that the leader should open the breakout group session by reviewing the assigned work and answering any questions participants might have).

- *Involving breakout group members in reporting.* The more the merrier is sound guidance where breakout group reporting is concerned. Within reason, as many members as feasible of each breakout group should report back in plenary session on the work accomplished, not only because involvement in reporting will make their experience more satisfying, but also because it will make the retreat more interesting. And since the board members leading the groups have already been involved in a highly visible, rewarding role, they don't need to be reporters.

- *Avoiding formal consensus or decision making.* Tying loose ends is far better handled after the retreat, as part of a well-developed follow-through process, so that participants can engage in free-flowing brainstorming during the retreat, generating as much content as possible in only a day together. Forcing participants to engage is some kind of process to reach formal consensus on particular points or to make decisions (such as "voting" with sticky dots to determine the ranking of particular governance issues) inevitably not only adds tension and reduces brainstorming, it can result in seemingly rational decisions that subsequently, on closer examination, look slap-dash and have to be revised.

- *Mapping out the follow-through process.* Making clear in the retreat design how following through on the retreat will be handled not only makes retreat participants feel confident that committing their time will yield concrete results, it also ensures a productive retreat. For example, a recent client's follow-through process included the facilitator's writing a report recommending next steps, review of the report by the board's governance committee, and presentation of the report to the full board by governance committee members.

- *Using a professional facilitator.* If the district's budget allows, retaining an outside consultant to assist the ad hoc committee in designing the retreat, to facilitate the retreat, and to prepare the follow-through report can pay important dividends. For one thing, a skilled facilitator can ensure that the retreat accomplishes its objectives while also actively engaging participants. For another, a consultant with in-depth governance expertise and experience can be a valuable resource in developing the follow-through recommendations, while also saving significant staff time.

The governance task force approach, which many districts such as the Ector County Schools (Texas) and the Teton County School District #1 (Wyoming) have employed, works well when full board involvement from the get-go is not a political necessity. It is normally chaired by the school board president and includes at least two other board members and the superintendent. However, in the case of very small boards of five or even fewer members, it makes sense to involve all board members on the task force (provided that the full board dedicates stand-alone meetings to the task force effort, without merely adding task force work to the regular board meeting). If provided with capable consulting assistance, the governance task force has proved to be a very efficient mechanism for fundamentally updating the board's governing design. Over the course of typically five to six meetings, the task force: identifies and assesses governance issues (for example, the absence of a contemporary committee structure corresponding to the board's major decision-making streams); develops design recommendations (such as putting in place a new committee structure); presents the recommendations to the full board in a special work session; and oversees implementation of the recommendations. As with the governance retreat, retaining a consultant with both extensive facilitation experience and in-depth governance expertise can help to ensure success.

DEVELOPING THE PEOPLE ON THE BOARD

Because, unlike the overwhelming majority of nonprofit organizations, school boards are elected rather than self-appointed, they can't make use of a very effective board human resource development tool: creatively shaping the board's composition by screening potential candidates to fill vacancies, using a profile of desirable attributes and qualifications (for example, many nonprofit boards look for new members who bring successful experience on other boards, who have ties to critical stakeholder organizations, and the like). School boards must, therefore, work with the members provided by the voting public, developing their governing knowledge and skills through such means as a well-designed orientation process for incoming members, as the following scenario illustrates.

The board president opened the orientation for the three new board members by thanking them for taking the time from their busy schedules to partic-

ipate in the orientation session and introducing her board colleagues serving as chairs of the board's two standing committees and the superintendent. She asked them to open their orientation folders and proceeded to walk them through some key documents: the board's governing mission; a functional description of the board's standing committees; the guidelines governing committee operations; the current governing targets that are used to evaluate board member performance; and a set of board governing policies, dealing with such matters as potential conflicts of interest, superintendent performance evaluation, and the procedure for scheduling building visits. After some discussion and a brief break, the president turned the session over to the superintendent, who briefed the new board members on district operations, including enrollment figures over the past five years, a description of the district's revenue sources, the current expenditure budget, a summary of the "Strategic Plan of Educational Advancement," the executive table of organization, and biographical sketches of her top lieutenants.

This is an excellent example of how many districts around the country have in recent years beefed up their processes for orienting incoming board members, primarily by adding substantial content relating to the board's governing role, policies, and structure, so that the new board members can hit the ground running, rather than slowly "learning the governing ropes" over the course of their first year on the board. And many school board governance or board operations committees annually update a formal program, with a dedicated budget, for the ongoing development of board members' governing knowledge and skills, including attendance at conferences and workshops, the circulation of books and articles dealing with board leadership, and the assignment of seasoned board members to serve as mentors to incoming members. Two other approaches to developing the school board as a human resource that have been successfully tested in recent years have taken board human resource development up a significant notch:

- Developing a set of board member governing expectations that a standing committee—typically governance or board operations—can use to monitor board member performance (for example, that board members are expected to attend all board and committee meetings; that they are expected to come to meetings having reviewed the board or committee packet and prepared to participate actively; and the like). The point of these processes is to counsel erring board members, since discipline isn't a viable option in the case of an elected board. The good news is that, based on my experience, the great majority of board members, wanting to do a credible governing job, respond positively to such standard-setting.
- Specifying in the formal guidelines governing the operation of the board's standing committees that committee chairs and members be regularly rotated, thereby ensuring that all board members have the opportunity to

build knowledge and expertise in the major governing areas, such as strategic and operational planning and performance monitoring, and that no long-tenured board members "own" particular functions.

DEVELOPING THE BOARD'S ROLE

It is nothing short of amazing that, despite the long history of nonprofit and public boards in this country—going back to the 1600s—many board members have a difficult time describing the work of governing in greater detail than such meaningless generalizations as "policy making" and "direction setting." In recent years, many nonprofit and public Strategic Governing Teams have helped to clarify their boards' governing role by putting together a high-level description of the board's primary governing functions and responsibilities—often called the "Board Governing Mission." Typically brainstormed in a governance retreat, adopted by the full board after a refinement process, and periodically updated by the board's governance or board operations committee, the Board Governing Mission includes such board functions as: playing a leading role in setting clear strategic directions and priorities for the district; making sure district plans include measurable performance targets that can be used to monitor district performance; ensuring that the district's public image is positive and that it maintains close and productive working relationships with key external stakeholder organizations; striving to ensure that the district possesses the financial and other resources to carry out its educational mission fully; appointing a qualified superintendent, reaching agreement with the superintendent on his/her executive leadership targets, and evaluating superintendent performance at least annually. You will find a real-life example in Exhibit A below: Ector County Independent School District Board of Trustees Governing Mission.

It was pointed out above that the board governing mission is an excellent orientation tool for incoming board members. Also, board-savvy superintendents and their boards have put the elements (governing targets) making up their formal governing missions to good use in mapping out the board's detailed governing processes—often in board standing committees, as I'll discuss in chapter 4. For example, if one of the mission elements is that the board "plays a leading, proactive role in district strategic decision making, and in setting strong, clear strategic directions and priorities for all educational and administrative programs and operating units," then the board's planning committee knows that one of its major responsibilities is working with the superintendent in developing some kind of strategic planning process that will engage board members proactively in setting strategic directions and priorities. And if another governing mission element is that the board "ensures that the district's image and relationships with key stakeholders are positive and that they contribute to the district carrying out its educational mission," the board community/stakeholder relations committee knows that one of its responsibilities is to work with the superintendent in fashioning image building and stakeholder relations strategies.

The board's governing mission often serves two other major purposes. One is public education and image building. I was, for example, in the audience at a Rotary luncheon a couple of years ago where the school board president and superintendent opened their presentation on district leadership by running over their board's governing mission. Chatting with the people at my table after the presentation, it was clear that they were impressed not only by the demanding role the school board played, but also that the board had taken the trouble to map out a detailed vision. The woman next to me confided that it would have made her life much easier on the social services board she'd been appointed to several months ago if she'd been handed a detailed description of the board's role, rather than trying to figure out her responsibilities over the course of several meetings.

EXHIBIT A: ECTOR COUNTY INDEPENDENT SCHOOL DISTRICT BOARD OF TRUSTEES GOVERNING MISSION

The Board of Trustees, as the governing body of the Ector County Independent School District:

- Serves as the steward and guardian of the District's values, vision, mission, and resources.
- Plays a leading, proactive role in District strategic decision making, and in setting strong, clear strategic directions and priorities for all of the District's educational and administrative programs and operating units, ensuring that student achievement is the District's ultimate "bottom line."
- Monitors the District's educational, financial, and administrative performance against clearly defined performance targets.
- Ensures that the District's image and relationships with key stakeholders are positive and that they contribute to the District's carrying out its educational mission
- Advocates for all students, the District, and public education generally in the legislative arena and other appropriate forums.
- Strives to ensure that the District possesses the financial and other resources necessary to realize its vision and carry out its mission fully in Ector County.
- Ensures that Board members are fully engaged in the governing process, that the resources they bring to the Board are fully utilized in governing, and that their governing skills are systematically developed.

- Takes accountability for its own performance as a governing body, setting detailed governing performance targets and regularly monitoring the Board's performance against these targets.
- Hires a Superintendent responsible for providing executive direction to ECISD, works in close partnership with the Superintendent, ensures that clear, detailed Superintendent performance targets are set, and at least annually evaluates Superintendent performance against these targets.

And the reader shouldn't underestimate the role of the board's governing mission in melding board members into a more cohesive governing team and culture, by making clear how the board's unique role differs from the missions of all other organizations within the district structure. And even though at first blush it might sound far-fetched, I've seen the board governing mission raise board members' collective self-esteem, hence making the governing experience more ego satisfying. Many, probably most, school board members spend their whole governing career without being able to describe their board's role in terms that make clear how critical and challenging their governing work is.

THE BOARD'S GOVERNING ENGINES

It'd been a power-packed planning and development committee meeting, leaving board members tired but satisfied. Over the course of their two hours together, they had:

- *Reviewed and fine-tuned the district's updated vision and values statements, which had been brainstormed in last month's strategic planning work session and fleshed out and refined by an ad hoc committee involving administrators, faculty, and community representatives, and which the planning and development committee would be presenting to the board at its next meeting.*
- *Reviewed the preliminary reports of two task forces the committee was overseeing—one assessing computer hardware needs in the two middle schools and the other to examine the pros and cons of various school foundation models that might be employed in raising new revenues for the district—and provided feedback on their next steps.*
- *Spent about an hour finalizing next year's budget preparation calendar, focusing on the agendas of two new board work sessions that the superintendent recommended the committee host and discussed how the committee would present the budget calendar at the next board meeting.*

You've just read about the demanding and tremendously important work of a real-life board planning committee. Twenty-five years ago, when I was starting out as a governance consultant, I didn't consider committee structure a top-tier governing concern; it struck me as a bureaucratic matter with little theoretical oomph that had more to do with discipline than substance. Now I number well-designed board standing committees among the top five determinants of a board's governing effectiveness. For one thing, by sub-dividing the complex work of governing into coherent streams of governing decisions and judgments, committees ensure that these decisions and judgments receive the detailed attention they merit (and that the board as a whole could not possibly give). And by enabling committee members to deal in-depth with governing judgments and decisions, committees are not only a source of board member satisfaction, but also governing knowledge and expertise.

Well-designed board standing committees also contribute to the superintendent's success by generating board "spear carriers" who by bringing major recommendations to full board business meeting (for example, the values and vision statements finalized by the planning and development committee discussed above) free the superintendent from having to draw on her line of credit in making action recommendations directly to the board herself. Another benefit of well-designed board committees is that they function as a bulwark against board involvement in essentially administrative matters (commonly called micromanagement).

So what do I mean by "well-designed" committees? The cardinal structural design rule—long enshrined in the management canon—is that form (structure) should always follow function (the work being performed). In practice, this means that committees should be designed to facilitate and support getting work accomplished; otherwise, there is a mismatch that is guaranteed to hinder performance. You'll recall the definition of governing in chapter 1: making decisions and judgments that flow along three broad streams: strategic and operational planning/budget development; performance monitoring; and external/stakeholder relations. Following the structure-follows-function rule, therefore, any nonprofit or public organization, including school districts, will want its board structure to consist of three committees: planning; monitoring; and external relations. Many school boards have established a fourth committee to handle coordination of the board itself, typically called "governance" or "board operations." Figure 3.1 depicts an increasingly common board structure reflecting the structure-follows-function design rule.

The strategic and operational planning committee is responsible for overseeing board member engagement in district planning, including development of the annual budget, and for recommending planning "products," such as an updated values and vision statement and the annual budget, to the board for review and approval.

The performance monitoring/audit committee is responsible for monitoring educational and financial performance and presenting performance reports at board meetings and also for overseeing the internal audit function, in

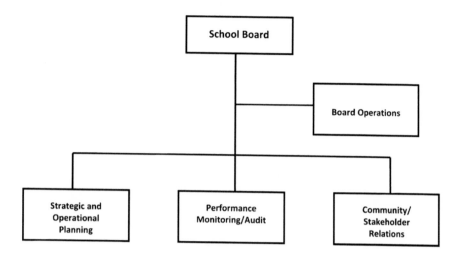

Figure 3.1. Standing Committee Organization Chart

this capacity ensuring that internal financial management systems are functioning properly. Another important function that is typically assigned to this committee is the review of new and updated district operating policies. And the community/stakeholder relations committee oversees the development of strategies to build the district's image and to ensure that its relationships with key stakeholder organizations are positive and productive.

The governance (or board operations) committee, typically chaired by the board president and consisting of the other standing committee chairs and the superintendent (as a non-voting member), carries out a number of critical functions: coordinating the work of the other standing committees; developing the full board meeting agenda; setting board member performance targets and monitoring board member performance; fashioning and executing a strategy for developing board member governing knowledge and skills; and maintaining a close, positive, and productive working relationship with the superintendent, including evaluating superintendent performance. In its capacity of standing committee coordinator, the governance or board operations committee usually typically updates and enforces a set of guidelines to govern committee operations and ensure their effectiveness, specifying, for example, that:

- All board meeting agenda items—both for information and for action—go through the standing committees.
- Committee chairs and members be regularly rotated among the committees.

- All reports at board meetings, other than the superintendent's, be made by committee chairs and members.

As noted above, well-designed committees that correspond to the actual governing work of the board are one of the most important bulwarks against the board's becoming involved in administrative details, wearing the dreaded micromanager hat. The reason is that committees organized around the actual work of governing keep the board focused on governing judgments and decisions. By contrast, the traditional "silo" committees that you might still see now and then in school districts actually encourage board micromanagement because they correspond to narrow programmatic and administrative streams of work that have nothing directly to do with governing, for example: personnel; finance; curriculum and instruction; and buildings and grounds. In effect, the old fashioned silo structure invites board members to become technical advisers rather than governors, thereby seriously diminishing the board's governing role.

In chapter 4, I'll describe in detail a very special and critical role of board standing committees: working closely with the superintendent and her top lieutenants in designing processes for board member involvement in the major governing areas—planning, monitoring, and external relations. Rapidly accumulating experience has taught that committees can very effectively play this "continuous governing improvement role," thereby providing the superintendent and top executives with a forum to work out the details of board engagement in a more informal, collegial atmosphere than the formal board business meeting.

ADAPTING TO SMALLER BOARDS

Since many school boards are relatively small (often only five to seven members), a structure of three committees plus the governance (board operations) committee will obviously not work well. For a board of seven members, a solution that has worked well in practice is to fold the community/ stakeholder relations committee into either the planning or performance monitoring committee, resulting in a structure of two "bread and butter" standing committees plus the governance or board operations committee.

For a tiny board of only five members, actual standing committees would sub-divide the board into units too small to have any credibility, so the practice of "virtual" committees has been successfully tested in recent years. A virtual committee is the board sitting as a committee of the whole, wearing the planning, performance monitoring, and community/stakeholders relations hats in separate sessions with a difference board member serving as chair of each virtual committee. For example, two weeks before the regular board meeting, the committee of the whole meets for, let's say, three hours: one hour as the planning committee; one hour as the monitoring committee; and one hour as the community/stakeholder relations committee. The virtual committees, while not as effective as full-fledged standing committee, do keep the board focused on the broad governing streams and, hence, guard into the board's slipping into micromanagement.

A CLOSING WORD ON STRUCTURE

As I have already observed, the great majority of board members are unpaid, part-time volunteers who find coming up with the time to attend committee and full board meetings enough of a challenge. So even armed with crystal-clear functional descriptions and qualified, dedicated members, board standing committees cannot be expected, on their own, to carry out their governing responsibilities in a full and timely fashion. Their success depends heavily on strong, well-planned, continuous support from the superintendent and her executive team. Many school districts and other nonprofit and public organizations have put formal committee support processes in place to ensure that board standing committees function as powerful governing engines that enable their boards do high-impact governing work. Two elements of these support processes have proved especially useful in practice:

- *The Chief Staff Liaisons*. The superintendent taps members of his executive team to serve as Chief Staff Liaison to each of the board's standing committees, in this capacity taking responsibility for ensuring—to the superintendent and executive team colleagues—that her committee successfully carries out its governing role. The Chief Staff Liaison: takes the lead in developing committee agenda items; oversees and coordinates the preparation of materials for committee meetings; makes sure that the committee chair is well-prepared to lead committee deliberations; and prepares the committee's report to the full board, typically employing a report template that the executive team has adopted.
- *Governance Coordinating Committee*. The Governance Coordinating Committee ensures adequate quality control of the committee support process. Chaired by the superintendent and consisting of her executive team members, the Committee meets, usually once a month, to: review and fine tune the committee agendas that are presented by the Chief Staff Liaisons; reach agreement on the assignment of committee preparation tasks (for example, preparation of a special report on community involvement for the board's community/stakeholder relations committee); review and revise the content of especially important documentation being sent to standing committees; and even provide an opportunity for executives to

rehearse presentations that will be made at upcoming standing committee meetings.

Chapter Four

Board Engagement in Governing Work

BOARDS THAT MAKE BETTER PARTNERS

As I've observed earlier more than once, school board members who are actively engaged in shaping their governing decisions and judgments derive greater satisfaction than board members who merely serve as a passive audience for finished staff work, making them more reliable partners for the superintendent in accomplishing the tremendously complex and demanding work of governing. Chapter 3 examined in detail one important way to foster active board member involvement in governing: building the board's governing capacity by updating its formal governing role, developing the people on the board, and putting in place a modern committee structure. This chapter describes a complementary approach to fostering active board engagement—employing the board's standing committee to tweak the processes for board engagement in major governing areas such as operational planning and budgeting and performance monitoring. As always, a board-savvy superintendent is in the thick of the action, assisting the board's standing committees in carrying out this process design function. This chapter also takes a close look at what I call the "gold standard" for board engagement: dealing with complex, high-stakes issues—both opportunities and challenges—that can't effectively be handled via business-as-usual operational planning.

GETTING A HANDLE ON BUDGETING

At one of the more interesting school board standing committee work sessions I've sat in on recently, the board's strategic and operational planning committee, along with the superintendent and associate superintendent for planning and development, spent 2 ½ hours finalizing the budget preparation process for the upcoming year, paying special attention to the board's involvement. Actually, the work session involved all five board members, sitting as the virtual strategic and operational planning committee of the whole. This was the second of two intensive sessions. At the first session, six weeks earlier, the virtual committee had spent a couple of hours reaching consensus on the key outcomes that committee members wanted the budget preparation process—and the budget document ultimately adopted by the board—to produce and on the issues that should be addressed in updating the budget preparation process.

The outcomes discussion that took place in the first work session had been eye-opening to committee members, who hadn't previously given much thought to outcomes that the budgeting process and the budget document itself were intended to produce, beyond the obvious need to have a detailed annual plan for district expenditures that were in balance with projected district revenues. As they brainstormed outcomes, it became clear that budgeting was a kind of Clydesdale of governing processes, with a powerful back capable of carrying a tremendous amount of valuable district luggage. For example, on the budget process front, committee members identified such outcomes as: clear, measurable district performance targets; the identification of major operational issues facing the district—both opportunities and challenges—and the development of innovative operational projects intended to address them within the annual budget framework (for example, putting together an innovative grant-funded program to promote more effective teaching of English as a second language in response to projected growth in non-English speaking students); and wider understanding among administrators and faculty of the factors driving expenditures. Two very important budget process outcomes were somewhat indirect but still critical: (1) the kind of strong board member ownership that could only come from proactive, creative involvement in the budget preparation process; and (2) a more cohesive internal culture as a result of wider faculty and administrator understanding of budget preparation details.

Brainstorming outcomes that the budget document itself might produce in the first work session was especially exciting since the question hadn't even been raised in the past. For example, everyone agreed pretty quickly that the adopted budget—at least in summary form—could be a powerful tool for educating the public at large and key stakeholders like the chamber of commerce and city and county governments on district priorities, goals, and finances. And they could see that, if properly presented, the budget document might also promote the district's image as a prudent steward of precious financial resources and as an efficient, well-managed public institution. It wasn't a big jump from local stakeholders to regional and national foundations, which might be more receptive to district funding proposals on the basis of a well-crafted budget document that painted a picture of an innovative, accountable, soundly managed educational enterprise.

The issues discussion in that initial budget process design work session of this district's virtual strategic and operational planning committee logically followed the outcomes brainstorming, since participants defined issues as current perceived gaps between the intended outcomes and what the budget process and document had actually produced in the past. For example, it hit everyone in the face that operational issue identification and performance target setting in the past had been a relatively minor, and largely ritualistic and cosmetic part of annual budget preparation—attached to the finished budget document at district headquarters at the end of the process, rather than driving in any way at all development of the line-item expenditure figures in the budget. No systematic attention at all had been given in the past to the funding of innovative operational initiatives as part of the budget process. Indeed, the process had basically consisted of principals—for their buildings—and district administrators—for their departments—merely updating expenditure spread sheets for the upcoming year, and the headquarters financial staff adding in updated cost drivers, such as projected utility increases.

The most dramatic issue identified in the initial strategic and operational planning work session was undoubtedly the absence of strong board ownership of the budget, as a result of the lack of creative, proactive board involvement in budget development. And it was patently obvious to work session participants in that initial session that the format of the budget document made it a virtually useless tool for educating—much less inspiring confidence among—funders, key community stakeholders, and residents. Easily weighing a pound and forbiddingly opaque, the budget to me largely consisted of seemingly endless rows and columns of numbers: the planned line-item expenditures for buildings and district departments. Opening with a brief, rather perfunctory discussion of district goals, the budget document was almost entirely an administrative document essentially aimed at control of expenditures. Anyone masochistic enough to spend the time to go through it would need a green eye shade and calculator.

Before taking a look at what happened at the second strategic and operational planning committee budget design work session, I'd like to consider the superintendent's role in this budget process design case. You'll be interested in knowing that the superintendent had approached the first committee work session with more than a little trepidation. Even though he'd apparently bought into the recommendation of the district's governance task force some eight months earlier to engage the board's standing committees in the design of board engagement processes in their respective functional areas, the superintendent hadn't really given the matter much thought until the first work session had been scheduled. In fact, the superintendent had let the committee design function fall by the wayside, and no strategic and operational planning committee work session would have been scheduled if the board president hadn't pressed him on the matter, as the superintendent admitted to me while we were chatting after the second work session.

At one of their biweekly lunch meetings, the president informed the superintendent that she and two other board members had grown so frustrated with the board's passive/reactive role in budgeting that they'd considered bringing it up in public at the last board meeting. Fortunately, before taking that dramatic step, which would have raised public questions about the superintendent's chief executive leadership, they had agreed that the president would raise the matter with the superintendent, who admitted at their lunch that he'd largely ignored the committee role in process design because he wasn't sure how it would play out in practice. As the superintendent confided to me in our chat after the second work session, every time he'd thought about sitting with one committee or another to engage in process design, it had felt like opening Pandora's Box. After all, it was a pretty revolutionary step in the context of traditional K–12 governance theory, with its unrealistic fire wall separating "pure" board work from "pure" administrative work. I recall the superintendent saying that he could imagine board members wreaking havoc by dabbling in the details of essentially administrative processes like budget preparation.

Pressure from the board president and two other board members left the superintendent no choice but to begin to engage committees in process design in their respective functional areas, but, I'm happy to report, this pretty board-savvy superintendent, once he was committed, didn't have to be dragged kicking and screaming into the committee design process. Rather, he consciously decided to build into the committee design process sufficient quality control to ensure that committee deliberations turned out to be productive and stayed on track. He would achieve this by serving as a strong consultant to the committees, wearing two hats: the designer and facilitator of committee process; and the expert adviser to the committees.

For example, in preparation for the first strategic and operational planning committee work session, the superintendent had worked with his associate superintendent for planning and development to map out a methodology that the committee could employ in brainstorming budget outcomes and in identifying budget process issues that needed to be addressed. He and his associate superintendent had then gone over the methodology with the committee chair, who accepted the superintendent's offer to facilitate committee brainstorming at the first work session. The superintendent had gone even further, discussing what appeared to be budget process-related issues with the chair so that the chair was better prepared to play a substantive role in the brainstorming process.

It's important to keep in mind that the superintendent, while wearing his facilitator and substantive expert hats, was playing a strong chief executive role, even though it was a pretty radical departure from the traditional stand-offish role that would have the superintendent merely deliver recommendations to board members for their review and approval. The superintendent confided to me that before the first committee work session, he'd been afraid that he'd look a bit wimpy and not in control and, hence, lose face with the committee, but was tremendously reassured after getting through the session successfully. In fact, he told me, he came out of that first session feeling energized and even more influential as a chief executive, albeit exercising this new-found influence less directly than the old-fashioned command-and-control model would have allowed.

I'll bring this true story to a close by describing what happened at the second design work session of the board sitting as the strategic and operational planning committee. Based on the outcomes and issues identified at the first work session, the committee, along with the superintendent and his top planning officer, tweaked the upcoming budget preparation process in significant ways, including two major advances. First, at a kick-off work session early in the budget process, involving all board members, the superintendent, and his executive team (the direct reports, including the associate superintendents and department directors), board members would have an opportunity to discuss major operational issues identified by executive team members that appeared to merit serious attention in the budgeting process (for example, inadequate building security in light of recent tragedies around the country). These issues would be massaged and refined by the strategic and operational planning committee and become part of the budget preparation instructions.

This kick-off session would also engage board members in reviewing and reaching consensus on key cost drivers and revenue projections presented by the district's chief financial officer, including: scheduled administrator and faculty salary and fringe benefit increases; projected enrollment; projected physical plant maintenance and utility costs; projected property tax and state subsidy revenues; among other items. Another key outcome of this kick-off work session would be a tentative set of district-wide performance targets—both educational and administrative—based on a draft set presented by the superintendent. Following through on the work session, the strategic and operational planning committee would refine and finalize the performance targets.

A second major advance worked out at the second design session related to the format of the budget document that would eventually be adopted by the board eleven months hence, aimed at making the document a far more effective tool for educating, and building support among, community residents and key local, state, and regional stakeholders. For example, a new introductory section would provide a basic orientation on the district in terms of: its values, vision, mission, and long-range goals; actual district educational performance information; current and projected enrollment (including demographic data); its employees; its physical plant; its revenue sources; and its administrative structure, among other things. An operational planning section would set forth the annual operating targets and describe operational issues being addressed in the annual operating plan. And immediately before the traditional line-item details would be a new section summarizing and depicting revenues and expenditures graphically.

CONTINUOUS GOVERNING IMPROVEMENT VEHICLES

The foregoing detailed account of the design work of a school board's strategic and operational planning committee is a perfect example of board standing committees serving as what you might call continuous governing improvement vehicles—annually tweaking the processes for engaging board members in the major governing streams: planning, monitoring, and community/stakeholder relations. Standing committees, unlike the full board meeting, provide board members and the superintendent with a relatively informal venue for working through complex process questions free of the intensive public scrutiny that accompanies board business meetings where formal decisions are made.

From the superintendent's perspective, engaging board members in process design work in committees helps to strengthen the board-superintendent working relationship, primarily because, in practice, board members are being invited to play a role in shaping their own governing work, in close collaboration with the superintendent. This is far from the traditional we-they approach in K–12 governance. By actively engaging with a board committee in tweaking governing processes, the superintendent also conveys that she is a self-confident chief executive who is not at all worried about potential board micromanagement.

Of course, as the strategic and operational planning committee story demonstrates, the governing improvement process depends on the superintendent's playing an active and assertive role, as both design facilitator and substantive adviser. For example, the superintendent paid close attention to the development of the agendas of both of the committee work sessions described above, ensuring that they would accomplish their goals, and also made sure that the committee chair was well-prepared to lead the deliberations. The superintendent also came to the second work session well-prepared with practical suggestions that the committee could consider in coming up with concrete budget process enhancements.

You can be sure that the superintendent didn't just sit back passively while the board members on the committee came up with all of the potential process tweaks. And as the above account also makes clear, the design process is guided by both technical and psychological aims. Technically speaking, the process being tweaked by one of the board's committees must ultimately work as intended (for example, a budget process that ultimately results in the timely adoption of a balanced line-item budget). Psychologically speaking, the process must involve board members actively enough and early enough to generate the degree of ownership that fuels strong board commitment to the ultimate product.

OTHER EXAMPLES OF GOVERNING PROCESS DESIGN

I have in recent years seen many board governance (or board operations) committees map out processes for coordinating, monitoring, and improving board members' governing performance, carrying out what I think of as the "board self-management" function. For example, the governance or board operations committees of many school boards have developed a set of board member performance expectations to use in monitoring governing performance. These are typically fairly simple, common sense indicators, such as: attending all full board and committee meetings; coming prepared to board and committee meetings; attending certain district functions, such as graduation ceremonies and faculty convocations; and adhering to formal guidelines that the school board has adopted for such processes as board member visits to school buildings and board member requests for information from the superintendent and her direct reports.

The good news, in my experience, is that the great majority of board members sincerely want to do a capable job of governing, welcome clear performance expectations, and tend to want to meet them. And, of course, since school boards are not self-appointing and possess little formal authority over their members, monitoring is always a somewhat sensitive process. What appears to work best is a very low-keyed approach, spending some time at every governance or board operations committee meeting discussing any performance issues that have arisen (most often failure to attend two meetings in a row) and following-up by having one of the governance committee members contact the erring member inquiring about the absences. Of course, the very rare serious ethical lapse (most often a perceived conflict of interest) requires a more formal response that might involve legal counsel.

With regard to the governing performance of the board as a whole, what has worked well in many districts is the governance or board operations committee holding an end-of-year work session at which the committee discusses what the board has accomplished over the past year, how full board meetings have gone, and how well the standing committees have functioned. Sometimes, board self-assessment information is brought into the discussion. For example, many boards have their members fill out a simple evaluation form assessing every board meeting. The bottom line of these end-of-year work sessions is the development of board development targets for the upcoming year based on the major performance issues identified in the work session.

The performance monitoring committees of many school boards also play an active role in upgrading their oversight and monitoring work, often at a special work session at the end of the year. As was true of the strategic and operational planning committee case above, the superintendent plays an assertive, substantive role in helping the committee come up with functional tweaks. To take a real-life example, the performance monitoring committee of a school board I worked with a couple of years ago tackled the issue of financial reporting in a three-hour work session that resulted in a far more effective process. The quarterly financial report had become a major issue since many board members found it confusing and totally inadequate as a tool for understanding the district's financial status at particular points in time. As one board member was quoted as saying, "I feel like I need to bring a calculator to meetings so I can figure out what the damn report is saying." The current financial report was a classic case of too much information, rather than too little: pages of detailed line-item expenditure information, with no obvious rhyme or reason.

What the committee came up with was a summary financial report using bar charts and PowerPoint slides to show actual versus budgeted expenditures by major cost categories—for the quarter just ended and year-to-date. The summary also included an analysis section explaining any developing expenditure issues, in a bullet-point format on the PowerPoint slides. Of course, the traditional line-item expenditure detail the board had always received was still provided in the board packet, but it was never discussed unless a board member who'd made an effort to go through the detailed backup document had a specific question. Since this board had adopted committee guidelines requiring that all reports to the board be made by committee chairs and members, the committee established a new custom when it approved the new financial reporting format: setting aside 15 minutes of every meeting when the financial report was being reviewed for the committee chair, or whoever on the committee would be presenting the quarterly report at the upcoming board meeting, to do a run-through of the PowerPoint slides.

The very board-savvy superintendent had strongly urged the committee to build this "dress rehearsal" into its meetings, knowing that if a committee presenter sounded uncomfortable or ill-prepared, it would damage the credibility of the report—and also of the committee structure. The superintendent was also keenly aware that if a committee presenter was allowed to do a less than capable job of presenting, it would be ego-deflating and could quite easily turn the embarrassed board member into a less reliable governing partner. By the way, in addition to a better-informed board, financially speaking, and satisfied committee members, one of the major benefits of the enhanced financial reporting process was increased public understanding of the district's finances, which over time, subsequent surveys showed, strengthened public support for the school system, which in the past had been seen by many community members as secretive and aloof.

Many school board performance monitoring committees have also in recent years enriched the process of monitoring educational performance, going beyond reviewing the results of state-mandated standardized testing and tracking drop-out rates. For example, one committee over the course of three work sessions added to its educational monitoring kit bag such information as: progress in carrying out strategies to boost teacher classroom performance; annual assessments of principal performance in terms of accomplishing formally-established building improvement targets; the results of pilot tests, for example, of a new ESL curriculum; and even information on graduates' postsecondary experience (specifically, the percentage still enrolled in postsecondary institutions two years after graduation).

THE GOVERNING GOLD STANDARD

The following scenario is becoming much more common in today's rapidly changing, always challenging world, which is forcing school districts all over the country to confront thorny issues in the form of both challenges and opportunities. Recognizing that they face a stark choice—either be changed, quite often traumatically, by the forces swirling around them, or take command of their own change—they're increasingly choosing the latter, more proactive course.

Sifting through the list of issues—both opportunities and challenges—facing the district, which had been identified at the daylong strategic work session involving all board members, the superintendent, and her top lieutenants two weeks earlier, the board's planning committee, working closely with the superintendent, came up with a short list of three issues that demanded very special attention now because they were too high-stakes and complex to be handled through the mainstream operational planning/budget development process and the cost of deferring action was deemed as prohibitive. One was clearly the most challenging: the need to close at least two elementary schools because of the steady decline in households with kids of school age—a decline that was projected to accelerate over the next five years or so. An issue of such technical and political complexity couldn't possibly be addressed through the mainstream operational planning/budget development process. Although a bit less daunting, the other two issues couldn't possibly have been handled through business-as-usual planning: the need to re-build

*the district's relationship with the business community, which had grown
extremely adversarial in recent years, especially because of an almost certain campaign two years hence to seek a real estate tax increase in light of
declining state subsidy; and an increasingly dysfunctional school board that
clearly needed to be transformed into a more cohesive governing body.*

*The vast majority of issues that had come up over the course of the day
together were operational, in the sense that they could effectively be addressed in putting together next years' operational plans and budget, for
example: needed tweaks to the faculty development plan and budget to capitalize on recent research on instructional methodology; the need to beef up
security at the middle school; and the need for a change in the contract with
the county literacy council for the use of school tutoring space to reflect
increased district utility and maintenance costs. These and the other operational issues were very important and demanded serious district attention,
but feeding them into the annual operational planning process made the best
of sense.*

Over the past decade a new approach to identifying and addressing complex, high-stakes issues that, like the three described in the above scenario,
can't be handled through the normal operational planning process—what are
commonly called "out of the box" issues—has been successfully tested and
is rapidly spreading in the public and nonprofit sectors, including K–12
education. Widely known as the "change investment portfolio process," this
approach is, in my professional opinion, the "gold standard" for school board
involvement in the planning function for four pretty obvious reasons. First,
the stakes involved in effectively addressing the issues are so high for the
district that they compel serious school board attention. Second, school board
members, drawing on their diverse knowledge, expertise, experience, community connections, and perspectives, are uniquely qualified to participate in
the portfolio process, particularly early-on in the issue identification and
selection phases. Third, since implementing significant change almost always encounters resistance and often requires a significant financial investment, school board involvement is essential for generating commitment. And
fourth, as every board-savvy superintendent well knows, it wouldn't be prudent from a psychological perspective to keep the school board on the pe-
riphery of such an important and exciting process.

Therefore, many board planning committees in recent years have worked
closely with their superintendent in designing applications of the portfolio
approach that are tailored to their district's unique circumstances. Although
in planning, as in almost all other functions, one size cannot possibly fit all,
these applications have certain features in common:

- The district holds a kick-off board-superintendent-executive team "strategic work session," at which district values and vision are revisited and

updated, issues are identified and analyzed, and possible change initiatives are brainstormed.

- The board planning committee analyzes the issues subsequent to the work session, and selects what appear to be out of the box issues. The issues that are clearly operational are then funneled to the annual operational planning/budget development process to be addressed.
- The board planning committee next analyzes the out of the box issues in greater detail in order to determine which ones need to be tackled at the present time, and which ones can be relegated to the "tomorrow file" to be dealt with in subsequent years. In practice, of course, the selection process is far from scientific, but it does take serious thought. The objective is to select the issues that appear to involve the highest cost to the district if not addressed in the near term—in other words, the price of not acting now on the issues. For example, referring back to the scenario opening this section, you can readily understand that failing to get started now with rebuilding the district's working relationship with the business community would jeopardize passage of the tax levy two years hence, since the rebuilding process could be expected to take a long time.
- Of course, the superintendent and her executive team are closely involved every step of the way, working closely with the board's planning committee, but at this point the ball is passed to the superintendent and her team, who take the lead in coming up with mechanisms for addressing the selected issues (for example, a task force consisting of top district administrators, parents, and community leaders to fashion a building closing strategy; a board governance task force to deal with the board dysfunction issue).
- The change projects that are generated to address the selected out of the box issues are separated out from mainstream district operations and managed in the change investment portfolio, where they will receive the attention required to ensure implementation.
- As the years pass, change projects in the district portfolio are implemented (or in some cases abandoned) and mainstreamed, while new issues are identified and new projects added to the portfolio.

BUT EXPECT THE UNEXPECTED

It would certainly be convenient if all of the highest-stakes issues facing a district could be identified at an annual work session like the one I described above, but, alas, the real world has a way of disrupting the most carefully designed processes. Issues—both opportunities and challenges—can confront a school district at any point in the planning cycle, and every now and then one will involve such high stakes and require such immediate attention that it can't wait for the next issue identification work session. This was certainly the case with the Hillsborough County Public Schools in Florida back in 2009, when Superintendent MaryEllen Elia received a call from a representative of the Bill and Melinda Gates Foundation, informing her that the district was being invited to compete for a grant up to as much as $100 million to foster teacher effectiveness. The grant would involve a huge infusion of resources into a district with little flexible money to invest in innovation, but MaryEllen knew that applying for the grant would be tremendously taxing in terms of staff time, although the Gates Foundation would be funding consulting assistance to the district in the application process. There was obviously no time to go through a lengthy planning process: either act now, or forgo the possibility of a $100 million infusion. MaryEllen acted, immediately going to her board to secure its go-ahead and putting together a special structure and process to prepare the grant application, including regular board oversight and monitoring.

What is the upshot of taking resolute action to capitalize on a tremendous opportunity? The Hillsborough County Public Schools received $100 million, which is supporting a wide-ranging seven-year innovation initiative, Empowering Effective Teachers, which consists of five core initiatives: (1) Measuring Teacher Effectiveness: involving a fundamental redesign of the district's teacher evaluation system and its linkage to professional development; (2) Performance-Based Career Ladder: involving the establishment of a career ladder that clearly defines the performance level required for tenure as well as the levels required for advanced roles; (3) Next Generation Pay-for-Performance: involving the fine-tuning of a teacher compensation system that awards large salary increases based on sustained performance and progress up the career ladder, rather than years of experience or credentials; (4) Programs and Incentives for High-Needs Students: involving the further development of policies and incentives to address both schools with a critical mass of high-needs students, as well as the 60 percent of high-needs students who are located in the highest-performing schools; and (5) Apprentice Teacher Acceleration Program: involving the implementation of a comprehensive, high-quality induction program aimed at addressing the high attrition rate among new teachers and accelerating their performance growth.

The change investment portfolio process is not intended to supplant traditional long-range operational planning for three or more years; its explicit purpose is to handle the kind of out of the box issues that cannot be addressed effectively by either annual or long-range operational planning. When it makes sense to project ongoing operations beyond a year in the future, then boards and superintendents should do so. A perfect example would be a long-range capital plan, including both renovation and construction. Another would be a long-range financial plan. That said, it is critical boards and superintendents do not confuse long-range planning with the portfolio process described above. They involve radically different purposes and methodologies.

AND ON THE NONGOVERNING FRONT

The primary mission of all boards is to govern, which is defined earlier in this book as making decisions about such governing products as the annual operating plan and budget and making judgments based on such information as a quarterly financial report and standardized test results. By its very nature, governing is somewhat aloof work, requiring some distance from the welter of day-to-day affairs in order to attain the degree of objectivity that sound decisions and judgments require. Many members of nonprofit and public boards, including school boards, are also involved in doing hands-on non-governing work, such as representing the school district in such district events as graduation ceremonies and in such external forums as the annual chamber of commerce luncheon meeting. There is absolutely nothing wrong with school board members doing such non-governing work, just so long as: (1) it is intended to help the school district achieve an important, board-recognized goal; (2) direct board member involvement makes good sense in terms of both district needs and board member qualifications; and (3) the non-governing work is not allowed to interfere with the board's preeminent responsibility: governing the district.

In fact, one of the most important reasons for a school board to make a standing community and stakeholder relations committee part of its governing structure is to ensure that non-governing board member involvement is well-conceived and productive. The stakes are especially high in the external relations arena, in light of the widespread and apparently growing distrust of public institutions, including public schools, and the growing reluctance to provide additional financial support in the form of local real estate taxes or state subsidy. Many people believe—and I certainly concur—that school board members are uniquely effective as external representatives of their districts. For one thing, their obviously important and highly visible governing role signals that our district cares enough to send you our very best for your event. For another, since school board members are in the vast majority of cases elected, they represent their district as "one of us," rather than as paid professionals who are seen the "they" side of the "we-they" division.

Many board community/stakeholder relations committees lay the foundation for productive board member involvement in external affairs by taking two very important steps: updating the district's formal image statement, identifying how the district wants and needs to be seen by the general public and stakeholders in order to carry out its educational mission effectively; and identifying and prioritizing key stakeholder organizations in the community.

Both of these steps are often taken in a special committee work session so that they receive the focused time and attention they deserve. The image statement, which consists of the key messages that the district needs and wants to send to the community, is normally brainstormed by completing the sentence "We need and want to be seen as," after which the image elements are refined and finalized and, in many cases, recommended to the full board for review and approval. Typical image statements include such elements as: "a prudent steward of public financial resources;" "efficient;" "driven by a fervent commitment to student achievement;" "transparent in our operations;" "dedicated to active parent involvement;" "providing a nurturing, secure learning environment for our students."

The obvious purpose of the image statement is to provide board members with talking points when they are out in the community representing their district. The point is to shape perceptions of the district, for the very simple reasons that good—even stellar—performance very often does not speak for itself and can easily go unnoticed by the general public and district stakeholders. Of course, actual performance trumps image building over time, and no amount of image building can make up for consistently poor performance. That said, aggressive image building is a sensible strategy in these skeptical times, when public institutions are generally viewed with suspicion that is not easily overcome.

Stakeholders are organizations, institutions, and formally organized groups with which it makes sense for a school district to maintain a working relationship because important stakes are involved. Typical school district stakeholders are city and county governments; chambers of commerce; civic organizations such as Rotary and Junior League; the print and broadcast media; economic and community development corporations; higher education institutions; and the state department and legislative committees overseeing K–12 education. A common approach that is used to prioritize stakeholders involves, first, brainstorming a comprehensive list of stakeholders, and, second, assessing the stakes involved in each stakeholder relationship. The relationships involving the highest stakes obviously call for the most district attention, including school board member representation at key stakeholder events, such as the annual meeting.

Many school board community/stakeholder relations committees oversee a robust board member "speakers' bureau," booking board members to speak at such functions as chamber of commerce and Rotary luncheons. In this regard, one of the committee's most important responsibilities, in addition to selecting the highest priority stakeholder forums, is to assure that speakers acquit themselves well at the podium, not only in terms of connecting with the audience and getting key points across, but also providing speakers with an ego satisfying experience (and sparing them the embarrassment that failing at the podium would cause). The key elements of the image statement I described above certainly provide important speaking points, as do current district priorities (such as the need to build community support for a capital improvements tax levy), critical district issues (such as the need to explain why two schools must be closed over the next two years), and notable district accomplishments (such as a significant improvement in test scores).

Beyond making sure that board speakers are armed with clear speaking points, committees also ensure board member success at the podium by providing them with slides when appropriate and even an opportunity to rehearse their presentations. On occasion, a board member might be joined at the podium by the superintendent or other senior district executive, most often when the issues being discussed are so complex that it would be unrealistic to expect a board member to explain them and field questions alone.

Other examples of important board member hands-on involvement in district external relations include:

- Representing the district on the boards, committees, and task forces of really high-priority stakeholders, such as a local development corporation's task force charged with fashioning a comprehensive business attraction strategy with a public education component or an ad hoc chamber of commerce committee responsible for improving communication between the business community and public schools. Since superintendents traditionally receive most if not all invitations to participate in stakeholder bodies, it is critical that the superintendent make a point of bringing such invitations to the board's community/stakeholder relations committee for discussion. And successful district representation requires clear committee direction and regular oversight to ensure that the best interests of the district are served by board member involvement. At the very least, board members representing the district should be provided with clear, detailed policy positions on issues under consideration in the external board, commission, or task force.
- Enlisting board members as advocates for the district, often in league with the superintendent or another district executive, for example: testifying about K-12 issues before a state legislative committee or commission; meeting with foundation staff to discuss a district funding proposal. By the way, since many foundations these days consider evidence of active board engagement in doing high-impact governing work when they make funding decisions, involving the board chair or one or more other board members in presentations to funders can help play a critical part in securing grants.

School board members can also play an important symbolic role internally in their district, for example by attending such functions as graduation ceremonies, by touring schools and visiting classrooms, and even by attending key meetings (for example, accompanying the superintendent to a meeting of a faculty task force presenting its preliminary recommendations for strengthening parental involvement in the buildings). Such symbolic internal involvement is one of many ways to create a more cohesive district culture, communicating to faculty and administrators that board members are colleagues in the educational enterprise, not just distant overseers who are watching over things to make sure that everyone is doing a good job—in other words, that the board is a vital part of the "we" making up the district, rather than outsiders foisted on the district by the electors.

Chapter Five

Maintaining a Healthy Board-Superintendent Working Relationship

.

NOT TAKING THE RELATIONSHIP FOR GRANTED

Up to this point, I have described the work of governing a school district in detail and explored three keys to building the kind of rock-solid school board-superintendent partnership that these challenging times demand:

- A board-savvy superintendent who brings a tremendously positive attitude to her work with the board, seeing it as a precious district asset, makes the governing function a top-tier chief executive leadership priority, and pays close attention to the human dimension of her relationship with the board
- A well-designed governing architecture consisting of board members who possess the requisite governing knowledge and expertise, a clear board governing role spelling out the board's major governing functions, and a board standing committee structure that corresponds to the actual flows of board governing decisions and judgments: planning; performance monitoring; and external/stakeholder relations
- And the use of board standing committees to continuously update the processes for engaging board members in making their governing judgments and decisions

There is no question that if school board members and superintendents pay close attention to these three keys, the odds of building and maintaining a close, positive, productive, and enduring board-superintendent Strategic Governing Team will be much more favorable. However, as pointed out in chapter 1, the board-superintendent working relationship is so fragile and so prone to erode, that keeping it healthy requires going beyond the three keys and focusing explicitly on the finer touches of relationship management. Never forget that board members and superintendents make for a combustible mix—a strong-willed, often opinionated cast of characters blessed with robust egos. Also keep in mind that school boards and superintendents are engaged in an extremely high-stress governing enterprise: making an unending stream of complex decisions in the context of a rapidly changing world, unremitting pressure from multiple constituencies that exert a centrifugal force on the board, and widespread suspicion and skepticism toward public institutions. It is nothing short of a miracle that so many board-superintendent partnerships last as long as they do and that so much good governing work is accomplished.

This chapter brings *Governing at the Top* to a close by examining four elements of an effective board-superintendent relationship maintenance program:

1. Make board-superintendent relationship maintenance an explicit function of one of the board's standing committees.
2. Fashion detailed board-superintendent communication and interaction guidelines.
3. Put in place a well-designed process for board evaluation of superintendent performance.
4. And build a strong board president-superintendent leadership team.

THE RESPONSIBLE COMMITTEE

A few years ago, I worked with a superintendent who was a virtuoso educational leader—an eloquent interpreter of her district's educational mission who cared passionately about student achievement and classroom performance and who was an outstanding leader of educational innovation in her district. But she didn't relish wearing another one of the important chief executive hats: manager-in-chief, making sure that well-designed administrative systems were in place and functioning effectively. Part of the problem was that she'd managed to climb the professional ladder to reach the top spot in her district without having to learn the managerial ropes, starting as a middle school teacher, becoming an assistant principal and then principal, and finally, before her appointment as superintendent, spending five years as associate superintendent for curriculum and instruction. Now ensconced in the superintendent's office, for her first couple of years she'd relied on her chief financial officer to play the chief administrative role and followed the "no news is good news" philosophy where administrative matters were concerned.

The inevitable result—underperforming administrative systems—had become a major problem in board members' eyes by the end of her second year, and her working relationship with the board was growing ever more tenuous. The board was especially concerned about the human resource management system, in light of increasing turnover and growing morale problems in several buildings. The issue of superintendent inattention to a critical facet of the chief executive role in the district could have continued to fester, and might well have ended this highly creative educator's CEO tenure, but for the timely intervention of her board's governance committee. In an intensive day-long session with the superintendent, the governance committee hammered out an agreement that she would devote far more attention to administrative matters, with special focus over the coming year on human resource management, including recruiting a new associate superintendent for human resources.

As this true life case illustrates, a board governance committee can serve a powerful relationship maintenance function. Chapter 3 described the role of a board governance or board operations committee, which typically consists of two major functions: (1) board coordination and management, including developing board member governing knowledge and skills, developing the board agenda, and coordinating the work of the other standing committees; and (2) managing the relationship with the superintendent, including ongoing monitoring of the relationship and resolving any issues that might pop out and conducting the annual superintendent performance evaluation. Typically headed by the board president and consisting of the chairs of the other board standing committees and the superintendent (as a non-voting member), the governance or board operations committee is the obvious candidate for management of this precious but fragile working relationship. Without an explicitly accountable committee of this kind, board-superintendent relationship issues can all too easily go unnoticed and be allowed to fester until the relationship is irreparably damaged.

COMMUNICATION AND INTERACTION GUIDELINES

Not long ago, a school board member I was interviewing told me a true story about flawed board-superintendent communication. This board member had been approached at the supermarket by a couple of constituents the week before, who were really interested in learning more about the multicultural dialogues that had recently been initiated at the middle school with funding assistance from the local community foundation to cover the cost of a facilitator. They had both heard the superintendent describe the initiative at a recent League of Women Voters luncheon meeting, where the superintendent was speaking on issues related to the increasingly diverse student population

in the district. As this angry board member related to me, she was speech-
less—literally—since she wasn't aware of the initiative. She was also tremendously embarrassed. When she called the superintendent about the inci-
dent later that afternoon, he, of course, was apologetic, explaining that he
was planning to brief the whole board about the initiative at the upcoming
board meeting. But this was clearly shutting the proverbial barn door after
the horse had escaped. This not-so-board-savvy superintendent had violated
a cardinal rule of effective board-CEO communication: The chief executive
should never let the board be caught off guard.

Open, honest, and frequent communication between the school board and
superintendent is without question an important means of keeping the working relationship healthy. In this regard, three communication channels that
have proved useful at the formal end of the spectrum include:

- Making sure that the superintendent's report at the regular board business
  meeting updates board members on developments that they should be
  aware of and are unlikely to have learned about through their committee
  work. The multicultural initiative described above would fit in this catego-
  ry. The superintendent's report is also an excellent vehicle for sharing
  with board members notable superintendent activities, such as meetings
  with the representatives of key stakeholder organizations such as the board
  of county commissioners, the CEO of the local community foundation, or
  the director of the state department of education, and attendance at state
  and national conferences.
- Using a weekly or bi-weekly superintendent e-letter to board members to
  summarize major developments the board should be aware of both inside
  and outside the district.
- And taking advantage of the less formal environment of the board's standing committee meetings to apprise board members of developments in the
  committees' respective functional areas.

Where formal superintendent communication with the board is concerned,
two general guidelines in addition to the golden rule of no surprises can help
to promote a more effective board-superintendent partnership: honesty and
openness; and relevance. The superintendent's credibility in the eyes of her
board members, and the level of trust in the relationship, depend more than
anything else on her always telling not just the truth, but the full truth—the
bad news as well as the good. Over the years, I have seen very few superintendents get into trouble with their boards by telling direct lies, but I have
seen many superintendents lose credibility by failing to make an effort to get
the full truth out, or by forcing board members to probe and dig to understand
an issue. The board-savvy superintendent makes sure that board members are
apprised of the full array of options available to them in dealing with an

issue, that they understand all of the important implications of making a particular decision, that they are alerted to the potential problem that is buried on page 6 of the quarterly financial report.

Formal superintendent communication should also be pertinent. Some of the best informed boards I have ever encountered are among the weakest at governing. Information is not, in itself, influence. The *right* information—meaning the precise information board members need to make decisions—is influence. As board members well know, effective communication involves much more than sending them pounds of paper; in fact, too much paper can detract from sound decision making. If the superintendent truly does care enough to send the board the very best governing information, he will think seriously about both content (is it the right information?) and format (is it easy to understand?). The classic case of terrible communication is the monthly financial report that is sent to many boards: columns and rows of numbers, page after page, requiring an accounting degree to decipher. Effectively communicating financial information means creatively summarizing, categorizing, and displaying the numbers so that the board can understand, without undue pain and suffering, exactly where the district stands right now in terms of actual versus budget expenditures by major cost centers.

Less formal communication can also help to strengthen the board-superintendent working relationship. Many board-savvy superintendents, for example, make a point of meeting one-on-one with every board member—often over breakfast or lunch—every couple of months at least, and, of course, more often with the board president. Informal meetings have proved to serve two very useful purposes. First, the board member and superintendent get to know each other at a more personal level. The old saw is definitely misleading. Familiarity, far from breeding contempt, narrows distance and facilitates bonding. The parties can't any longer see each other as cardboard stereotypes. Second, informal meetings encourage board members to share concerns and issues they are not likely to bring up in a more formal setting, especially if they are assured of confidentiality. Other kinds of informal communication that breed familiarity and, hence, foster closer working relationships are informal lunches or suppers before or after board meetings, where no discussion of governing work is allowed, holiday get-togethers, and summer picnics. My counsel: the more the better.

Having the board's governance or board operations committee adopt and keep updated a set of interaction guidelines is an important way of heading off issues that might seriously damage the board-superintendent working relationship. Two guidelines have proved to be especially helpful in keeping the board-superintendent partnership healthy:

- Only the board as a whole, speaking in one voice, can provide direction to the superintendent, and the board president is no exception. One of the

surest ways to add tension to the relationship is to allow the board president or any other board member give the superintendent direction of any
kind. Without this minimal safeguard, it is easy to imagine a superintendent getting caught in the untenable position of doing the bidding of a
particular board member who is at odds with one or more of her board
colleagues.

- Individual board members can directly ask for information from the superintendent or one of her direct reports, provided that assembling and reporting the information can be handled as a routine matter, requiring only a
  few minutes of time and not seriously disrupting the responder's schedule.
  An example that came up recently in a governance committee meeting I
  attended was a board member driving to a speaking engagement who
  called an associate superintendent to obtain the most recent drop-out sta-
  tistics for her presentation.

It would obviously be untenable for the superintendent to be put in the
position of enforcing observance of these and other interaction guidelines,
which clearly falls within the purview of the governance or board operations
committee. As a practical matter, only board members can police their peers,
and only via a formal committee, never as individuals.

SUPERINTENDENT EVALUATION

One of the most important functions of a high-impact governing board that
takes seriously its fiduciary responsibility to the wider public is to regularly
evaluate the performance of its superintendent. An effective process for
board evaluation of superintendent performance is also one of the most powerful vehicles for maintaining a healthy board-superintendent working relationship. Many school boards, in my experience, do this critical job poorly,
and some not at all. Some board members apparently avoid superintendent
evaluation because it feels negative and makes them uncomfortable, and
others because they have no idea how to do it well. Board-savvy superintendents are well-aware they can't afford to let their board avoid evaluating their
performance, or to do a shoddy job at it, because a well-designed and rigor-
ously executed evaluation process is one of the most important keys to a
healthy, productive, and enduring board-superintendent partnership.

From the superintendent's perspective, an effective board evaluation process also helps to ensure greater job security. If the superintendent's performance is not regularly and effectively assessed by the board, she stands a far
better chance of becoming the victim of shifting political alliances on her
board or of highly subjective judgments that are not performance-based.
Merely urging the board to carry out its evaluation responsibility will not, of

course, suffice. A poorly designed evaluation might be worse than none. Six characteristics of evaluation processes that have proved to be very effective include: (1) a responsible board standing committee; (2) the use of negotiated "CEO-centric" leadership targets to measure superintendent performance; (3) active, intensive board-superintendent dialogue; (4) a focus on education and growth; (5) documented formal consensus; and (6) full board information and input. Each of these characteristics will be briefly examined, and then I will take a detailed look at the negotiation of "CEO-centric" superintendent performance targets.

One of the more important ways of ensuring that the evaluation process is taken seriously is to make one of the board's standing committees accountable for making sure that the process is well designed and for actually carrying out the evaluation. The board's governance or board operations committee is the most obvious candidate since it is already accountable for management of the board-superintendent working relationship. In light of its membership—typically headed by the board president and including the other committee chairs—the governance or board operations committee brings special insights and credibility to the evaluation process.

Of course, a staple of the evaluation process is the assessment of overall district performance, using the targets set in the annual operating plan and budget as the measuring stick. However, equally if not more important in measuring superintendent performance are the superintendent's "CEO-centric" performance targets that have been negotiated with the governance or board operations committee. The problem with the popular functional checklist approach to evaluation (e.g., assessing superintendent performance in carrying out such open-ended functions as "serving as a spokesperson for the district" or "strategic planning," employing a scale of, say 1 to 5) is that it trivializes the evaluation process, is terribly subjective while appearing to be precise, and more often than not misses the point. Objectivity—and fairness—can only be achieved by basing the superintendent's evaluation on the extent to which well-defined performance targets that are directly linked to the annual operating plan and to the superintendent's CEO leadership role have actually been achieved. Whether or not the superintendent is "good" at public speaking, financial planning, or some other general function would be irrelevant even if it were possible to measure performance in the absence of specific targets. This facet of the evaluation process is so critical to its effectiveness that I discuss it in some detail in the following section.

The stakes involved in board evaluation of superintendent performance are so high, and the subject matter of CEO-ship so complex that the governance or board operations committee should commit substantial time—in formal session—to discussing how fully each of the negotiated CEO-centric performance targets has been achieved. To prepare for the formal session, each committee member should do an in-depth evaluation of the superintendent's performance in achieving each of the negotiated targets. However, given the complex nature of the superintendent's CEO work, the evaluation process should amount to more than merely tabulating the individual results and coming up with a summary document that is presented to the superintendent. Active dialogue with ample give-and-take are in order as committee members present their individual evaluations. The superintendent must be an active participant in the process, for both substantive and ethical reasons. It would be unconscionable for the governance or board operations committee to complete an evaluation and just hand it to the superintendent.

Evaluation is not intended to be a negative or punitive process. Rather, it is a tremendous educational opportunity for both the board committee and superintendent, who can use the process to learn not only about each other's perspectives, but also about the nature of CEOship itself. If seriously conducted, the evaluation process inevitably leaves its participants more knowledgeable about the district CEO leadership function. It is also intended to result in the superintendent's professional growth by indicating performance areas that need to be beefed up. In this regard, one of the outcomes of the process should be explicit agreement on the steps that the superintendent will take to strengthen performance, the timetable for taking action, and the board support that will be provided. For example, I worked with a superintendent whose board agreed that if he was to make a greater effort to build ties with key stakeholders in the community, he should be able to hire an associate superintendent to oversee internal administrative affairs.

The governance or board operations committee should reach formal agreement on both the evaluation and the superintendent's follow-through action plan, and both should be incorporated in a document that committee members and the superintendent sign. Although a board as small as five members might handle the evaluation as a committee-of-the-whole sitting as the governance committee, it does not normally make sense to involve the whole board in depth. However, it is important that, at the very least, the formal, written evaluation and the superintendent's action plan to address shortfalls are shared with all board members and that they be given the opportunity to offer comments and suggestions before they are finalized.

A DETAILED LOOK AT CEO-CENTRIC PERFORMANCE TARGETS

I worked with a superintendent a few years ago who had been brought into the district with a mandate from her board to get the organization into shape from a business perspective. Over the course of three years, this was her all-consuming task, and she delivered—in spades. A new financial management system took advantage of state-of-the-art computer support to supply administrators and the board with accurate and timely financial reports that made monitoring the district's financial status far easier than when she arrived on the scene. The budget preparation process was significantly upgraded, new purchasing policies and procedures were instituted, and contract management was at last put on a sound footing. The ship was now in superb shape. However, just about the time the superintendent had accomplished much of what she had been charged to do, her working partnership with the board had become seriously frayed, and several board members were quietly—behind the scenes—talking about her possible dismissal.

It turned out that this was a classic case of changing board expectations that had not been articulated to the superintendent, who, as far as she knew, was doing exactly what she had been charged to do when she had been appointed three years earlier. To be sure, four new trustees (out of a total of nine) had joined the board over this period, but they had not made a point of questioning the superintendent's priorities. Her style was brusque, and she did not suffer fools gladly, but the board had never discussed the matter of style with her. Her preoccupation with internal administrative system development had left a vacuum on the external front, and some key stakeholders in the community were feeling neglected, including the CEO of an influential family foundation that had supported several school programs over the years and the president of the chamber of commerce, which featured the school district in its business attraction strategy. However, she had never discussed priorities in the external arena with the board. There were also rumblings of discontent in the faculty ranks because the prior superintendent had been far more of an educational philosopher than his successor, who paid little attention to the articulation of lofty educational goals, but the board had never explicitly asked her to wax more eloquently on matters of educational philosophy.

Stories like this are not uncommon in my experience, and they probably end unhappily in most cases, with the wounded superintendent being sent packing without understanding what went so wrong so fast. The problem is usually a mismatch between many board members' expectations as to superintendent priorities and performance targets and the superintendent's understanding of those expectations. This kind of dangerous misunderstanding can fairly easily be prevented. One of the most important ways to ensure that the superintendent's understanding of the board's expectations as to her priorities and performance targets as CEO—and one of the keys to keeping the partnership with the board healthy—is to annually negotiate CEO-specific performance targets with the board, as a critical part of the foundation for effective board evaluation of superintendent performance. These targets are above and beyond the district-wide educational, administrative, and financial performance targets that are re-set every year through the annual operational planning and budget preparation process. They relate to the superintendent's priorities as an individual and the superintendent's use of his CEO time, rather than to the whole school district.

CEO-ship is a highly complex profession in all organizations, including school districts, requiring that multiple roles be balanced: partner with the board in governance; educational leader; top administrator; district spokesperson and diplomat to stakeholder organizations. In the context of a rapidly changing world that presents school districts with a constantly changing array of leadership challenges calling for CEO attention, the superintendent's leadership priorities will necessarily evolve. Last year's superintendent CEO leadership priorities may not fit this year's circumstances. If the board and superintendent take the time every year to sit down together to discuss the changing challenges and the implications for CEO priorities and to establish new CEO-specific performance expectations, no expectations gap is likely to develop.

Of course, in keeping with its evaluation responsibility, the board's governance or board operations committee should be accountable for negotiating the CEO-centric performance targets with the superintendent. Categories that have proved useful in this regard are:

- *Support for the board*: What are the superintendent's targets in terms of promoting and supporting more effective board leadership for the district? For example, will the superintendent devote considerable time to making sure that the new standing committee structure is fully functional within the first six months of the new academic year?
- *External relations*: What are the superintendent's targets in terms of promoting the district's public image generally and more specifically in terms of building ties with key stakeholders in the community? For example, will the superintendent pay special attention to repairing a frayed relationship with the local economic development corporation, which has become a vocal critic of the district over the past several months?
- *Educational leadership*: What are the superintendent's targets in terms of strengthening the district's educational programs to meet changing student and community needs and to capitalize on changing technologies? For example, will the superintendent become the champion of curriculum reform aimed at better preparing students to thrive in today's increasingly wired world?
- *Financial resource development*: What are the superintendent's targets in terms of strengthening the district's financial condition, including maximizing and diversifying revenues? For example, will the superintendent personally take on the challenge of building a nonprofit "schools foundation" with a board of prominent business leaders that will actively seek corporate and other grants to promote educational innovation?

- *Internal operations and system development*: What are the superintendent's targets in terms of promoting operational efficiency and building an internal climate that is conducive to carrying out the educational mission fully? For example, will the superintendent spend significant time in the coming year meeting with faculty in the various buildings, listening to their concerns and exploring practical ways to address them?
- *Individual professional development*: What are the superintendent's targets in terms of strengthening his or her professional standing and professional skills? For example, will the superintendent ask for board approval to participate in the six-week leadership development program of a major university this coming summer?

Now, having read this discussion of superintendent-centric priorities and performance targets, distinguished from district-wide performance targets, many readers are probably asking themselves, "Isn't he inviting the board to cross the line into purely administrative matters? After all, any self-respecting superintendent should be able to handle the allocation of her own time, without board meddling." My answer is very simply: Yes, this recommended approach does cross a traditional line between "policy" and "administration"—but it is a misleading demarcation that can cause no end of trouble for boards and their superintendents when it is inflexibly enforced.

Keep in mind that, as the district's CEO, the superintendent is the board's closest partner in providing leadership to the district and is also the board's most precious human resource. The superintendent's leadership priorities are, without question, the board's business, and those priorities only have meaning in terms of the superintendent's use of her time. Granted, no superintendent would want his board members to begin managing his calendar, critiquing his time management skills, but at a broad level, board members should be invited to discuss the superintendent's broad allocation of time to key priorities. Otherwise, it would be impossible to reach meaningful agreement with the board on CEO-centric performance targets.

For example, I once worked with a superintendent who, in a meeting with her board's governance committee, proposed that she devote fully one-third of her time over the coming academic year to rebuilding faculty morale and commitment. Wearing her educational leader hat, she would personally facilitate faculty meetings in the different buildings, focusing on classroom issues and needs, and she would personally work with a task force of faculty that she would charge to address administrative support issues. She made clear to executive committee members that wearing her educational leader hat so prominently over the coming year would be at the expense of another priority, external relations, to which she proposed devoting significantly less time than last year. Particularly, she suggested that the joint school district-chamber of commerce initiative on business involvement in the schools be set back six months. The superintendent's CEO time allocation at this level, which often involves significant tradeoffs, is clearly not only the board's business, but also in the superintendent's best professional interests.

Another line that is often too inflexibly observed when considering the superintendent's CEO leadership targets is the one distinguishing between *what* the superintendent intends to accomplish and *how* she will go about accomplishing it. Many readers have undoubtedly heard people say that a school board should focus only on outcomes and let the superintendent handle getting them accomplished. In theory, this sounds sensible. Who would want a school board actively involved in putting together the superintendent's detailed implementation plans, much less shadowing him during the day? But in practice, board-savvy superintendents know that they must be willing to blur the line in the process of reaching agreement with the board on expectations, because the what and the how are more often than not intertwined and inseparable, particularly where the superintendent's leadership style is concerned.

For example, if one of the superintendent's top priorities this year—explicitly negotiated with the board—is to reinvigorate an administrative staff demoralized by major cutbacks resulting from failure of the property tax renewal levy eighteen months ago, the superintendent cannot expect to accomplish much by barricading himself in his office, issuing written exhortations periodically. He will have to be out there pressing the flesh, engaging people personally, at least understanding if not really feeling their pain. The choice is between leadership styles—the how—but it makes good sense for the superintendent to discuss this how question with the governance committee when negotiating leadership targets, for four compelling reasons. First, the style choice involves significantly different allocations of superintendent time. Second, the choice really will make a major difference in terms of superintendent impact and ultimate achievement of the goal: a reinvigorated administrative staff. Third, when the superintendent is dealing with leadership questions, which are far more a matter of art than science, she *does* need the advice and counsel of her leadership colleagues on the board. They are the peer group with whom the superintendent should be working out such questions. And fourth, such open and candid dialogue will help to cement the superintendent's bonds with the board, signaling not only her respect for, and trust in, board members, but also her self-confidence and lack of defensiveness.

I understand that fuzzying lines that some commentators describe as hard and fast and non-negotiable will feel dangerous to some readers. Welcome to the world of leadership at the highest level, where creativity and flexibility are far stronger virtues than mere discipline and the protection of perceived administrative prerogatives! Superintendents must keep in mind that even though it might feel like they are opening Pandora's box when they engage in detailed dialogue with their board on the use of their time and the choice of leadership style, they will put themselves in far greater danger by standing back, inside the boldly drawn line, keeping their board at a distance. Such standoffishness will not only make any agreement on the superintendent's CEO leadership priorities and targets less meaningful and firm, it will also deprive the superintendent of valuable counsel and of the more intense inter-action that would help to cement her relationship with the board.

THE BOARD PRESIDENT-SUPERINTENDENT LEADERSHIP TEAM

Finally, the school board president-superintendent working relationship is a critical piece of the overall board-superintendent partnership building puzzle, primarily because of the president's formal authority and influence in the governing realm. Serving as, in effect, the board's "CEO," the president is in a good position to either assist the superintendent in cementing his working relationship with the board or, as sometimes happens, to impede the develop-ment of a close and productive board-superintendent partnership. Recogniz-ing this, board-savvy superintendents never fail to make developing an effec-tive working relationship with their board president a top-tier priority.

The strongest board president-superintendent partnerships I've observed over the years have been actively developed and supported by really board-savvy superintendents, who understand that it would be unrealistic to expect a board president, who is by definition a part-time volunteer, to play the leading role in relationship building. The board-savvy superintendents who succeed at building solid working relationships with their board presidents: (1) bring a very positive attitude to their working relationship with their president; (2) take the trouble to get to know their president in-depth; (3) reach agreement with their president on the basic division of labor between these two key district leaders; (4) make sure that their president succeeds as chair of the board; and (5) help their board president achieve his or her professional objectives. This is what the board president can and should expect from her superintendent.

In my experience, the closest and most productive board president-super-intendent partnerships are promoted and supported by a board-savvy superin-tendent who really wants the board president to be his close "governing ally," and these superintendents are firmly committed to playing a proactive role in building and maintaining the alliance. They don't, on the one hand, merely sit back passively and let the partnership evolve. Nor, on the other hand, do they take a defensive approach aimed at preventing whatever board president happens to come along from meddling in their executive "business." Allow me to paraphrase what I've heard these savvy superintendents say about their partnership with the board president:

> I really want my board president to be in my corner—a close partner whom I can count on to be my advocate and champion with the board on issues close to my heart. I see the two of us as a real leadership team, with both of us playing a significant leadership role. One of my most important superintendent responsibilities is to think creatively about my president's leadership role and potential accomplishments and to map out a strategy for supporting my president in playing this role successfully. Sure, there's always potential for conflict, but the more I strategize about our partnership, and devote time and attention to keeping it healthy, the less likely we'll end up at loggerheads.

The school board president can validly expect that her superintendent will make a serious effort to understand her in various ways. Board-savvy superintendents recognize that the better they know their board president, the more successful they're likely to be in building and maintaining a positive and productive partnership. Take, for example, the superintendent of a large, rapidly growing school district in the Southwestern United States who has had notable success in building effective partnerships with her school board presidents over the years. She makes a point of spending several hours with every new president early in his or her tenure—usually over several breakfast and lunch meetings—becoming thoroughly acquainted with her new colleague at the top. One major benefit of this early, very intensive interaction is personal bonding with her new president. Knowing that friendship is a powerful lubricant, this board-savvy superintendent really does aim to develop a relationship with every one of her board presidents that is more than strictly business-focused, without ever threatening professionalism. What this board-savvy superintendent wants to know early in her relationships with her various board presidents relates to leadership style, personal professional interests and objectives, and ego needs.

Her various board presidents over the years have varied dramatically in the ways they learn and apply knowledge in arriving at conclusions and making decisions. For example, one of her brightest and most ambitious presidents wasn't a reader, and it wouldn't have been helpful to supply him with a written briefing exploring the pros and cons of a complex issue, such as re-drawing school district boundaries. So, although this board-savvy superintendent was highly comfortable with written communication, and a superb writer to-boot, she adapted by making sure she and this particular chair spent ample face-to-face time working through issues. It proved to be a sound strategy for both educating him and getting his support on important issues, and, by the way, it also earned his appreciation. Of course, other presidents over the years have demanded—and received!—beautifully crafted memoranda setting out options and offering recommendations. In her mind, her board president is always a key stakeholder to be satisfied, and adapting to differing learning and decision-making styles is a pretty inexpensive way of turning presidents into satisfied stakeholders.

As this board-savvy superintendent is also keenly aware, her board president's leadership style also relates to his public role. Over the years, she's encountered board presidents who want to play a visible and assertive role in getting the school board to make critical decisions, and who see themselves as—at least for the truly high-stakes issues—as spear carriers and change champions for the superintendent. When this is the case, our board-savvy superintendent has always gone out of her way to take advantage of this style, always cautioning her chair, of course, not to come across too strongly and preempt standing committees or alienate other board members. By contrast, when she's working with a school board chair who doesn't relish an up-front role but, instead, is more comfortable facilitating deliberations and working behind the scenes on consensus building, she adapts to this very different style. *She never, ever tries to fit the proverbial square peg in the round hole!*

This board-savvy superintendent also pays close attention to learning about her board presidents' passionate professional interests, what they really want to achieve as board president—the imprint they want to leave—and what matters to them ego-wise. Her mission is, within reason, to provide her presidents with opportunities for in-depth involvement in areas that especially interest them (for example, special education; performing and fine arts programming), to help her presidents to achieve their major professional objectives (for example, becoming a more accomplished public speaker; to become active in the state school boards association); and to find ego satisfaction where it matters (for example, the need to be seen as an educational statesperson; the need for media attention). Since I'll be discussing this dimension in more detail later, suffice it to say at this point that our board-savvy superintendent is keenly aware of the levers that need to be pulled to cement her relationship with her board presidents, and she pulls them.

One really board-savvy superintendent of a large Midwestern district learned after a few years in the top spot that many, if not most, new board presidents that are elected to work with him will bring only a vague understanding of the presidential role to the partnership, and every now and then a new president will arrive who is just plain wrong-headed about the role. For example, he's had new presidents who see themselves as essentially in a ceremonial role with no responsibility for the board's governing decisions and judgments, and he's had chairs who—wrong-headedly and dangerously—see themselves as a kind of co-CEO. This board-savvy superintendent makes it a point very early in the relationship with his new board president to sit her down for a detailed, very explicit discussion of the basic division of labor between the two and the fundamental ground rules. He wants his president to understand—and agree—that:

- The board president is essentially the chair and "CEO" of the board—and only the board, in this capacity responsible for leading its governing deliberations.
- The superintendent is responsible for all internal operations of the district.
- And the external/community relations turf is a shared president-superintendent responsibility, requiring a carefully negotiated division of labor and considerable collaboration.
- Certain rules of the game will help to ensure a sound working relationship, including, among others, that: (1) Only the board as a whole can give direction to the superintendent, never the board president alone; (2) The whole board, or a designated committee of the board, is responsible for evaluating superintendent performance, never the board president alone; (3) The board president never gives direction to staff under the superintendent; and (4) Neither the board president nor the superintendent ever take public positions on major issues without the formal concurrence of the full board.

The superintendent I have been discussing, along with many other board-savvy superintendents, in my experience, have learned that it is very useful to have this fundamental division of labor and set of interaction guidelines formally adopted by the whole board and incorporated into a board "operating manual" of some kind. Otherwise, there will be a clear and present danger that a wrong-headed but very aggressive and persuasive board president can blur the lines and cause real trauma. I've seen board president-superintendent working relationships come to grief in the external relations area because the division of labor remains vague. One really board-savvy superintendent of a large suburban district in the Southeast has put together the following strategy, which has proved very effective in practice:

- She discusses in detail early in her board president's tenure what facets of the external relations agenda her president is most interested in: being booked to speak on behalf of the district in such forums as the monthly Rotary or chamber of commerce luncheon meeting? Participating in important meetings with critical stakeholders, such as the mayor or community college president? Being involved with the media, for example, being interviewed by newspaper reporters or participating in radio or TV public affairs panels? Presenting workshops at the annual state school boards association meeting or at national meetings? And so on.
- She reaches agreement with her board president on a schedule of external relations "engagements" that they will handle separately or together (for

example, submitting a proposal to present a workshop at the next annual NSBA conference).

- She makes sure that her president is provided with the support he or she needs to succeed in representing the district in various forums (for example, an attractive set of PowerPoint slides for the Lions luncheon meeting; a thorough briefing paper before a press interview).
- And she is always on the lookout for new opportunities for her president to represent the district in the external world (for example, a call comes from the county executive's office asking the district to designate someone to represent it on the new countywide economic development commission being put together). One of the superintendent's little golden rules is that she never just accepts an invitation for herself without thinking about the board president first.

The board-savvy superintendent of a mid-size urban district in New England makes a point of preparing his board president for regular board business meetings, knowing that letting him sink or swim in leading board deliberations would be a high-risk course of action. His strategy includes:

- Running over the tentative agenda of the upcoming board meeting with the president before discussing it with the board governance committee, where it is finalized.
- Making sure his president thoroughly understands any complex agenda items that will be introduced at the board meeting so that he or she can be an effective facilitator of discussion.
- And also drafting a regular board president's report, describing the president's external activities on behalf of the district since the last board meeting.

Making his board president look "in command" at every board meeting has proved to be a critical ingredient in the glue cementing this precious, high-stakes partnership.

Another board-savvy superintendent I've worked with makes a point of knowing what his board president wants to achieve professionally from his or her unpaid service as the board's leader, and he goes out of his way to help his president achieve these objectives, recognizing that such non-monetary compensation is a powerful relationship builder. For example, one of his presidents had higher political aspirations, but wasn't a very effective performer at the lectern in large public meetings. This board president, knowing that his inadequacies as a public speaker would be a serious barrier to his long-term political success, shared his need for help with the superintendent, who made a real effort to help his president become a capable, if not outstanding speaker, by making sure he was "booked" to speak regularly (beginning with smaller, safer venues), supplying him with presentation aids such as PowerPoint slides and handouts, and actually making sure he had opportunities to rehearse and receive constructive feedback.

Another of this superintendent's presidents—an entrepreneur who had built a highly profitable computer services business—shared his keen interest in countywide economic development, not only because he was passionately interested in the county's economic and social well-being, but also because significant population and job loss over the past couple of decades threatened the bottom line of his own company. So the superintendent did some behind-the-scenes lobbying to secure his president's appointment to the county workforce development board, and when the county administrator invited the superintendent to serve on the newly formed countywide economic development commission, the superintendent put forward his president's name instead.

About the Author

President & CEO of Doug Eadie & Company, **Doug Eadie** has over the past quarter-century helped more than 500 public and nonprofit organizations, including many public school districts, to build rock-solid board-chief executive leadership teams, do truly high-impact governing, and take command of strategic change. Eadie is the author of twenty books in addition to *Governing at the Top*, including *The Board-Savvy Superintendent*, *Extraordinary Board Leadership: The Keys to High-Impact Governing*, and *Five Habits of High-Impact School Boards*, and of more than 100 articles. A Phi Beta Kappa graduate of the University of Illinois at Champaign–Urbana, Doug received his master of science in management degree from Case Western Reserve University. Before founding Doug Eadie & Company, he held a number of senior executive positions in the public and nonprofit sectors and served for three years as a Peace Corps teacher in Addis Ababa, Ethiopia.

CPSIA information can be obtained at www.ICGtesting.com
Printed in the USA
BVOW07s0435240114

342850BV00001B/1/P